Praise for *The Best American Poetry*

"Each year, a vivid snapshot of what a distinguished poet finds exciting, fresh, and memorable: and over the years, as good a comprehensive overview of contemporary poetry as there can be."

—Robert Pinsky

"*The Best American Poetry* series has become one of the mainstays of the poetry publication world. For each volume, a guest editor is enlisted to cull the collective output of large and small literary journals published that year to select seventy-five of the year's 'best' poems. The guest editor is also asked to write an introduction to the collection, and the anthologies would be indispensable for these essays alone; combined with [David] Lehman's 'state-of-poetry' forewords and the guest editors' introductions, these anthologies seem to capture the zeitgeist of the current attitudes in American poetry."

—Academy of American Poets

"A high volume of poetic greatness . . . in all of these volumes . . . there is brilliance, there is innovation, there are surprises."

—*The Villager*

"A year's worth of the very best!"

—*People*

"A preponderance of intelligent, straightforward poems."

—*Booklist*

"Certainly it attests to poetry's continuing vitality."

—*Publishers Weekly* (starred review)

"A 'best' anthology that really lives up to its title."

—*Chicago Tribune*

"An essential purchase."

—*The Washington Post*

THE
BEST
AMERICAN
POETRY
2016

◇   ◇   ◇

Edward Hirsch, Editor

David Lehman, Series Editor

SCRIBNER POETRY

NEW YORK   LONDON   TORONTO   SYDNEY   NEW DELHI

Scribner Poetry
An Imprint of Simon & Schuster, Inc.
1230 Avenue of the Americas
New York, NY 10020

First Scribner edition September 2016

For information about special discounts for bulk purchases,
please contact Simon & Schuster Special Sales at 1-866-506-1949
or business@simonandschuster.com.

The Simon & Schuster Speakers Bureau can bring authors to your live event.
For more information or to book an event, contact the Simon & Schuster Speakers
Bureau at 866-248-3049 or visit our website at www.simonspeakers.com.

Manufactured in the United States of America

1   3   5   7   9   10   8   6   4   2

Library of Congress Control Number: 88644281

ISBN 978-1-5011-2755-7
ISBN 978-5011-2756-4 (pbk)
ISBN 978-1-5011-2757-1 (ebook)

CONTENTS

David Lehman was born in New York City, the son of Holocaust survivors. Educated at Stuyvesant High School and Columbia University, he spent two years as a Kellett Fellow at Clare College, Cambridge, and worked as Lionel Trilling's research assistant upon his return from England. He is the author of nine books of poetry, including *New and Selected Poems* (2013), *When a Woman Loves a Man* (2005), *The Daily Mirror* (2000), and *Valentine Place* (1996), all from Scribner. He is the editor of *The Oxford Book of American Poetry* (Oxford, 2006) and *Great American Prose Poems: From Poe to the Present* (Scribner, 2003), among other collections. Two prose books appeared in 2015: *The State of the Art: A Chronicle of American Poetry, 1988–2014* (Pittsburgh), comprising the forewords he had written to date for *The Best American Poetry*, and *Sinatra's Century: One Hundred Notes on the Man and His World* (HarperCollins). *A Fine Romance: Jewish Songwriters, American Songs* (Schocken) won the Deems Taylor Award from the American Society of Composers, Authors, and Publishers (ASCAP) in 2010. Lehman teaches in the graduate writing program of the New School and lives in New York City and in Ithaca, New York.

FOREWORD

by David Lehman

◊   ◊   ◊

If our age is apocalyptic in mood—and rife with doomsday scenarios, nuclear nightmares, religious fanatics, and suicidal terrorists—there may be no more chilling statement of our condition than William Butler Yeats's poem "The Second Coming." Written in 1919, in the immediate aftermath of the epoch-ending disaster that was World War I, "The Second Coming" extrapolates a fearful vision from the moral anarchy of the present. The poem also, almost incidentally, serves as an introduction to the great Irish poet's complex conception of history, which is cyclical, not linear. Things happen twice, the first time as sublime, the second time as horrifying, so that, instead of the "second coming" of the savior, Jesus Christ, Yeats envisages a monstrosity, a "rough beast" threatening violence commensurate with the human capacity for bloodletting.

Here is the poem:

> Turning and turning in the widening gyre
> The falcon cannot hear the falconer;
> Things fall apart; the centre cannot hold;
> Mere anarchy is loosed upon the world,
> The blood-dimmed tide is loosed, and everywhere
> The ceremony of innocence is drowned;
> The best lack all conviction, while the worst
> Are full of passionate intensity.
>
> Surely some revelation is at hand;
> Surely the Second Coming is at hand.
> The Second Coming! Hardly are those words out
> When a vast image out of *Spiritus Mundi*
> Troubles my sight: somewhere in sands of the desert
> A shape with lion body and the head of a man,

A gaze blank and pitiless as the sun,
Is moving its slow thighs, while all about it
Reel shadows of the indignant desert birds.
The darkness drops again; but now I know
That twenty centuries of stony sleep
Were vexed to nightmare by a rocking cradle,
And what rough beast, its hour come round at last,
Slouches towards Bethlehem to be born?

As a summary of the present age ("Things fall apart; the centre cannot hold; / Mere anarchy is loosed upon the world"), stanza one lays the groundwork for the vision spelled out in stanza two, which is as terrifying in its imagery as in its open-ended conclusion, the rhetorical question that makes it plain that a rough beast is approaching but leaves the monstrous details for us to fill.

As an instance of Yeats's epigrammatic ability, it is difficult to surpass the last two lines in the opening stanza: "The best lack all conviction, while the worst / Are full of passionate intensity." The aphorism retains its authority as an observation and a warning. Think of the absence of backbone with which certain right-minded individuals may be said to have met the threats of one bloody ism or another since the 1930s. Or consider our self-doubt and shaken confidence today, our lack of unity, the stalemate between rival factions. (In at least one sense, our House is divided against itself.) On the opposite side, jihadists and advocates of Sharia are rightly known for their extreme zealotry. All totalitarian regimes are based on dogma, and all dogmas demand of their followers a "passionate intensity" capable of overwhelming all other considerations.

Yeats works by magic. He has a system of myths and masks—based loosely on dreams, philosophy, occult studies, Celtic legend, and his wife's automatic writing—that he uses as the springboard for some of his poems. In a minute I will say something about his special vocabulary: the "gyre" in line one and "*Spiritus Mundi*" eleven lines later. But as a poet, I would prefer to place the emphasis on Yeats's craftsmanship. Note how he manages the transition from present to future, from things as they are to a vision of revolution and destruction, by a species of incantation. Line two of the second stanza ("Surely the Second Coming is at hand") is syntactically identical with line one ("Surely some revelation is at hand"), as if one phrase were a variant of the other. It is the second time in the poem that Yeats has managed this rhetorical maneuver. The first occurs in the opening stanza when the "blood-dimmed tide" replaces the "mere anarchy" that is "loosed" upon the world. In both cases the second line intensifies the first by substituting something specific for something abstract or general.

The phrase "the Second Coming"—when repeated with the addition of an exclamation point—is enough to unleash the poet's visual imagination just as, in "Ode to a Nightingale," the word "forlorn" concluding the poem's penultimate stanza returns at the start of the final stanza, governing the dramatic final transition in Keats's poem. In "The Second Coming" the bestial image that follows, "A shape with lion body and the head of a man," is all the more terrifying because of the poet's craft: the metrical music of "A gaze blank and pitiless as the sun"; the unexpected adjectives ("indignant desert birds," "slow thighs"); the haunting pun ("Reel shadows"); the oddly gripping verb ("Slouches"); the rhetorical question that closes the poem like a prophecy that doubles as an admonition.

In a note written for a limited edition of his book *Michael Robartes and the Dancer*, Yeats explained that "*Spiritus Mundi*" (Latin for "spirit of the world") was his term for a "general storehouse of images," belonging to everyone and no one. It functions a little like Jung's collective unconscious and is the source for the "vast image" in "The Second Coming." Yeats writes in his introduction to his play "The Resurrection" that he often saw such an image, "always at my left side just out of the range of sight, a brazen winged beast that I associated with laughing, ecstatic destruction."

As for "gyre" (pronounced with a hard *g*), in Yeats's system it is a sort of ideogram for history. In essays on Yeats I have seen the gyres—two of them always—pictured sometimes vertically, in the shape of an hourglass, and sometimes horizontally, as a pair of interpenetrating triangles that resemble inverted stars of David. The gyre represents a cycle lasting "twenty centuries."

But I maintain that knowledge of the poet's esoterica (as set forth in his book *A Vision*) is, though fascinating, unnecessary. Nor does the reader need to know much about falconry, a medieval sport beloved of the European nobility, to understand that there has been a breakdown in communications when the "falcon cannot hear the falconer."

Read "The Second Coming" aloud and you will see its power as oratory. And ask yourself which unsettles you more: the revolutionary monster "slouching toward Bethlehem" or the sad truth that the best of us don't want to get involved, while the worst know no restraint in their pursuit of power?

I have begun my foreword with Yeats's poem for two reasons. The first is that I can think of few works so eerily prophetic—and so apt for us today. The second is that we who work on *The Best American Poetry* mean to honor the great poems of the past even as we celebrate the vitality of verse in our time.

★ ★ ★

Edward Hirsch was my choice to edit the anthology this year because my admiration of his poems is matched by my respect for his skills as a critic, a teacher, and a judge—all that goes into the editing of an annual anthology that does its best to promote the art itself and showcase some of the poems that have moved or amused us. When Kobe Bryant announced his retirement from basketball with a poem, I thought of "Fast Break," one of the highlights of Hirsch's *Wild Gratitude* (Alfred A. Knopf), which won the National Book Critics Circle Award in 1986. "Fast Break" consists of one sentence stretched across thirty-six lines beginning with a hook shot that "kisses the rim and / hangs there, helplessly, but doesn't drop" to the other side of the court where the power-forward makes his lay-up but falls to the floor "with a wild, headlong motion / for the game he loved like a country // and swiveling back to see an orange blur / floating perfectly through the net."

In his career as a professor (at the University of Houston) and as president of the Guggenheim Foundation, Eddie has found a way to blend the tasks of pedagogy and critical judgment while relentlessly pursuing his passion for poetry. He has won widespread acclaim most recently for his book about the death of his son, *Gabriel: A Poem* (Knopf, 2014). At the same time he has written about poetry in essays and reviews, columns filed on a weekly deadline (*The Washington Post*), and an ambitious *Poet's Glossary* (Houghton Mifflin Harcourt, 2014); he has found time to edit a slender volume devoted to the nightingale in poetry, to introduce an anthology emanating from the Academy of American Poets' Poem-a-Day project, and to keep a demanding travel schedule. We compared notes and enthusiasms frequently and I know it gave him great pleasure that a significant number of poets in this volume have never previously appeared in *The Best American Poetry*.

Important poets have died in the last two years. Philip Levine, C. K. Williams, Claudia Emerson, and James Tate are four whose work appears in this year's *BAP*. I feel a special sorrow at the passing of Jim Tate, who was the guest editor of the 1997 volume. I got to talk to Jim on the phone regularly during the whole of 1996 and felt like a partner in the making of a brilliant anthology. He was real—he spoke mildly but knew what he wanted poetry to do. In his own work he was funny, very funny—funny, seemingly without effort. He helped people realize that humor is as compatible with the lyric impulse as the metaphysical wit of seventeenth-century poets such as Donne and Marvell. And he continually widened the possibilities of poetry in prose.

My favorite memory of Jim is from early May 2001. Jim and Dara Wier had organized and were hosting the Juniper Festival at the University of Massachusetts in Amherst. They invited me to be the keynote speaker. One evening Dara hosted a party at her place and invited my wife, Stacey, and me to come. I asked Jim for directions. "Would you like me to draw a map for you?" he asked.

"That would be good," I said.

"Look at my palm," he said, turning up his right hand and using a left-hand finger as a pointer.

I looked at his palm and suddenly we were in a James Tate poem.

"Do you see this line?" he said.

"Yes," I said. "It's your lifeline."

"Well," he said, "you go up this line and then you hang a left up here."

"How long will it take?" I asked.

"Not long," he said.

And the amazing thing is . . . on the basis of these directions . . . we got there. Safe and sound.

Edward Hirsch was born in Chicago in 1950 and educated at Grinnell College and the University of Pennsylvania, where he received a PhD in folklore. *For the Sleepwalkers* (1981), his first collection of poems, received the Delmore Schwartz Memorial Award from New York University and the Lavan Younger Poets Award from the Academy of American Poets. *Wild Gratitude* (1986), his second book, won the National Book Critics Circle Award. Since then, he has published seven additional books of poems: *The Night Parade* (1989), *Earthly Measures* (1994), *On Love* (1998), *Lay Back the Darkness* (2003), *Special Orders* (2008), *The Living Fire: New and Selected Poems* (2010), and *Gabriel: A Poem* (2014), a book-length elegy that received the National Jewish Book Award. He is the author of five prose books, including *A Poet's Glossary* (2014), *Poet's Choice* (2006), and *How to Read a Poem and Fall in Love with Poetry* (1999), a national bestseller. He taught for six years in the English department at Wayne State University and seventeen years in the creative writing program at the University of Houston. He is now president of the Guggenheim Foundation. He has received a MacArthur Fellowship, an Ingram Merrill Foundation Award, a Pablo Neruda Presidential Medal of Honor, the Prix de Rome, and an Academy of Arts and Letters Award. He lives in Brooklyn, New York.

INTRODUCTION

by Edward Hirsch

◇ ◇ ◇

The lyric poem has been practiced for more than four thousand years, and yet its history is still unfolding today. It is very much alive. It has been spoken, chanted, sung and written, compacted and compressed, expanded and enlarged. It has been pictorialized on tablets, inked into papyrus, typed onto paper, generated in virtual space. It is a nonutilitarian form of language sometimes put to utilitarian ends, used to build nations and to undermine them, to reinforce power and to protest it. In our era, it has been radically wrenched and questioned, turned and twisted, stretched nearly beyond recognition, reframed, reformed, hybridized, ecologized, politicized, erased—its difficulties are notorious—and yet it continues to speak from the margins, to move and tell stories, to disturb and console us. It engages our interior lives, social experiences, planetary woes.

There are so many whirling crosswinds in contemporary American poetry, so many voices and schools vying for attention in our cultural noise that it can be difficult to sort things out, to understand the various issues at play. Some of the conversation around contemporary aesthetics is serious, much of it distracting or frivolous. What is the principle of our work, what is the task, what is at stake for poetry now? I have often turned to the history of poetry to try to comprehend our current situation. Perhaps it can also help us figure out where we are going.

Lyric poetry has its roots in the Egyptian hieroglyph and the Chinese ideogram, the Hebrew letter, the Greek alphabet. The Greeks defined the lyric as a poem to be chanted or sung to the accompaniment of a lyre (*lyra*), the instrument of Apollo and Orpheus, and thus a symbol of poetic and musical inspiration. It emerged from religious ritual, tribal practice. "Poetry everywhere is inseparable in its origins from the singing voice and the measure of the dance," the linguist Edward Sapir writes. The first songs were most likely created to accompany occasions of celebration and mourning. Prayer, praise, and lamentation are three of the oldest subjects of poetry. We still recognize them in various forms, such as psalms, odes, and elegies.

Aristotle distinguished three generic categories of poetry: lyric, drama, and epic. This categorization evolved into three types or classes determined by who is supposedly speaking in a literary work. The lyric, a poem uttered through the first person, was distinguished from the drama and the epic or narrative. It took the form of monodies, sung by individuals, or choral odes, simultaneously sung and danced by a group of performers.

The lyric, especially the monody, was counter-posed against the epic. Whereas the speaker of the epic acted as the deputy of a public voice, a singer of tales narrating the larger tale of the tribe, the speaker of the monody was a solitary voice speaking or singing on his or her own behalf. The lyric poem thus opened up a space for personal feeling. It introduced a subjectivity and explored our capacity for human inwardness. The intimacy of lyric stood against the grandeur of epic, its exalted style and heroic themes, its collective nostalgia. The short poem asserted the value and primacy of the singular witness. Here was the quotidian and the sublime. Ever since Longinus cited it as a supreme model of poetic intensity, we recognize the ferocity of Sappho's poem of jealousy, her lyric meltdown *phainetai moi*. And I can still hear the chirping of a cricket under the window of a Chinese poet a thousand years ago.

The textbook division between lyric, drama, and epic is helpful but flawed. "Like all well-conceived classifications," the Portuguese poet Fernando Pessoa writes in "Toward Explaining Heteronymy," "this one is useful and clear; like all classifications, it is false. The genres do not separate out with such essential facility, and, if we closely analyze what they are made of, we shall find that from lyric poetry to dramatic there is one continuous gradation. In effect, and going right to the origins of dramatic poetry—Aeschylus, for instance—it will be nearer the truth to say that what we encounter is lyric poetry put into the mouths of different characters."

The lyric shades off into the dramatic utterance. Poems become dramatic when we get the sensation of someone speaking, when we hear a poem, in Robert Frost's words, "as sung or spoken by a person in a scene—in character, in a setting." That can be the case even when the author seems to be speaking in his or her own voice. "When I state myself, as the Representative of the Verse," Emily Dickinson cautioned Thomas Higginson in a letter, "it does not mean—me—but a supposed person." That's why Dickinson's assertion is as true for Robert

Lowell and Sylvia Plath, so-called confessional poets who intentionally collapsed the distance between the persona and the writer, as it is for Robert Browning, the master of what he termed "dramatic lyrics," and Ezra Pound, whose book *Personae* established the masks at the center of his work. Creating a persona, even a close or naturalistic one, is a way of staging an utterance, and there is always a difference between the writer who goes to work and the speaker who emerges in the text. In poetry, selfhood is a constructive process.

Writing fixes the evanescence of sound and holds it against death. During the Renaissance, English writers began to write their lyrics for readers rather than composing them for musical performance. The words and the music separated. Song is vestigial, but writing offers a different space for poetry. It inscribes it, whether in print or on a screen, and thus allows it to be read, lingered over, reread. It also gives the poem a spatial dimension, a defined visual as well as auditory life. It appeals to the eye as well as to the ear. And it appeals to unique as well as common experience. Poetry becomes, as Allen Grossman asserts, "a principle of power invoked by all of us against our vanishing."

Poetry gives us the logic of imagination. Neither a form of visual art nor a mode of music, it borders both, moving toward concrete visualizations on one side, the materiality of language (think of pattern poems), and soundscapes on the other, something meant to be listened to, heard, beyond language (think of wordless verse). It has elements of the fictive, the subjective, the irrational, and taps deep into the well of the unconscious. It can be broken down into its constituent parts, to sounds and syllables, to nonsense words, which may have a shamanic power. "If we think of the soul as split between the government of intellect and a stormy population of feelings," the Russian futurist Velimir Khlebnikov wrote in his essay "On Poetry" (1919), "then incantations and beyondsense language are appeals over the head of the government straight to the population of feelings, a direct cry to the predawn of the soul. . . ."

As contemporary American poets, we are inheritors of the modernist impulse in poetry, a lacerated language. We recognize as our own an acutely self-conscious mode of writing that breaks the flow of time, leaving gaps and tears. We grew up on the discontinuous texts of modernism, collages and mosaics, fragmentary structures, such as *The Waste Land*, a poem without a fixed center, without a single narrator or narrative thread to hold it together. It contains scenes and vignettes from a wide variety of times and places: agitated scraps of conversation, parodies, intertextual allusions, unattributed and often drifting quotations—a dark medley of radically shifting languages, a disturbing cacophony of voices. There is also "The Bridge," Hart Crane's full-scale reply to Eliot, a kind of broken epic, a "mystical synthesis" of the American past, present, and future, a wavering embrace of contemporary life. We internalized the recurrent strategies of the modernist poets, their many ways of using asyntactical, nonlinear language to create new semantic relationships. We studied their ruptures. We shored these texts against our ruins.

We are also inheritors of postmodernism in poetry. We have taken as a salutary corrective the idea that language is the author of any work of art; all narratives can be split open and deconstructed; what seems determined by nature is actually determined by culture. Reality is a construction, everything is interpreted. Postmodernism ultimately takes a skeptical position that denies the existence of all ultimate principles and truths, leading to an ironized attitude toward experience. We have been challenged and stimulated by its distrust of universalities, its misgivings about theories and ideologies, its commitment to indeterminacy, undecidability. In his "Postscript to *The Name of the Rose*," Umberto Eco distinguishes between the avant-garde, which historically wanted to deface and destroy the past, and postmodernism, which "consists of recognizing that the past, since it cannot really be destroyed, because its destruction leads to silence, must be revisited: but with irony, not innocently." There is no privileged or objective position from which to speak. We question the stability of truth. Since we are working in the wake of postmodernism, I would say that there is an even greater vertigo in contemporary poetry, a more extreme destabilization, sometimes cool and giddy, sometimes desperate for insight.

And yet it is also striking how many contemporary American poets experiment with the various traditional forms of poetry, the different shapes a poem can take, some prescribed or fixed, others organic. The poetic line still matters as a basic unit of meaning, a measure of attention, and the stanza, sometimes symmetrical or isometric, sometimes asymmetrical or heterometric, is still one of our most compelling ways of structuring a poem. There is fuller recognition now that the very division of poems into lines and stanzas has always created logical leaps and fissures, which distinguish poetry from prose. It is disjunctive, like a torn papyrus, and can accelerate with dizzying speed. Words floating in air, lines cut on a page, stanzas carved into units. Poetry is a mode of associative thinking that takes a different route to knowledge than philosophy, its ancient antagonist. It follows its own wayward but resolute path. Or as John Keats wrote to his friend Benjamin Bailey in 1817: "I have never yet been able to perceive how any thing can be known for truth by consequitive reasoning."

Our poets today are more eclectic than ever and draw on a plethora of sources, high and low, popular and literary. It may be that these divisions no longer apply. Surface and depth collapse. We employ the discontinuities of collage, its elisions and dramatic juxtapositions. And we also draw on more discursive modes of poetry, a way of putting things in rather than leaving them out, rapidly associating, making connections. Some poets adopt more narrative strategies, taking time as their latent or underlying subject. They do not fully narrate a story so much as they infer or imply one. Other poets, taking a cue from Wallace Stevens's late poems, such as "Notes Toward a Supreme Fiction," have created a more meditative and inclusive poetry of consciousness.

As a result, the old modernist and postmodernist divisions now seem a bit anachronistic. The various schools, the polemical "isms," which defined so many twentieth-century poetry skirmishes and battles, are on the wane. One can read syncretically, combining, say, William Carlos Williams, Elizabeth Bishop, John Berryman, George Oppen, James Wright, Gwendolyn Brooks, and Frank O'Hara. Is there a single poet who isn't influenced by poets from other languages, poets they read in translation, such as Rilke, Cavafy, and Celan, Miłosz, Herbert, and Szymborska, Akhmatova, Tsvetaeva, and Mandelstam, who believed that poetry is a form of recognition and that poets of all ages echo each other? What about Lorca, Vallejo, and Neruda, what about Bashō, Rumi, and Mirabai, what about the poets of the Tang Dynasty, such as Li Po and Tu Fu? What about Darwish, the breath of a people, and Césaire, the instigator of Négritude? I love the severe austerities of Montale, the reckless metaphors of Amichai, whose tenderness is startling. Apollinaire still seems utterly fresh to me, and I think often of his verdict on "that long quarrel between tradition and invention / Order and Adventure" ("The Pretty Redhead"). I wish I could talk to Stephen Berg again about his versions of the Hungarian poet Miklós Radnóti, and Mark Strand about his translations of the Spanish poet Rafael Alberti. We choose our own ancestors, our own influences—or perhaps they choose us. Everything, everyone, is potentially part of the mix. "The fact is that each writer *creates* his own precursors," Borges teaches us in "Kafka and His Precursors." "His work modifies our conception of the past, as it will modify the future."

The old divides, many of them holdovers from the 1960s, no longer seem relevant. Does anyone still need to choose between, say, image or narrative, metrical or free verse, traditional or nontraditional forms? Projective Verse, Deep Image, Naked Poetry—these are all part of our inheritance. It is no longer necessary to select exclusive anthologies, singular traditions. We could use a more synthetic reading, a more encompassing and inclusive history, of the poetic past. Poetry is not a competitive sport with different teams playing against each other. Does anyone still remember Philip Rahv's description of American literature as a cultural split between patrician writers, who moved in "an exquisite moral atmosphere," and rebellious frontier spirits, so-named "palefaces and redskins"? That language comes from another century.

The commitment to an individual voice, an unauthorized testimony, an eccentric viewpoint, is still one of the things that I value most about American poetry. In our age of suspicious reading, we no longer trust the claims of lyric poetry—its faith in the first person, its sense of a unified form, its very musicality—and yet some of our poets continue to write out of desire and experience, constructing things with urgency, out of necessity. They respond to our existential perils and predicaments, our hesitations, our uncertainties. They move between speech and song, combining lyrical and narrative values, inventing and describing things, formalizing them, referring to other poems, learning from other poets far and wide, those who have come before us, and seeking a personhood.

There is nothing like reading hundreds of literary magazines, thousands and thousands of poems in a given year, to unsettle and clarify one's judgment. I am grateful to David Lehman for our illuminating exchanges about the poems. One tries to be disinterested, but all reading is subjective. What was I looking for?—I wasn't always sure. What I found myself responding to, what continued to compel me, was precision and surprise. Memorable lines, craft deployed. Poems I could not shake, texts that arrested me. Poems that demonstrated a certain kind of thinking, imagistic or metaphorical thinking, poetic inquiry. Literary investigations, obsessions, intelligence. Emotional accuracy. Poems written under pressure, poems in which something dramatic is at stake, at risk, for the speaker, who would not be deterred. A kind of ruthless authenticity. Poems that take themselves to task. Poems in which something spooky or unexpected happens in language, poems that stood up to rereading, experiences I could not forget, the happiness and suffering of others. There are many poems of grief and lamentation here, but also erotic poems of celebration, comic poems of wild hilarity, odd joy.

I am proud to stand behind the poems in this book, an array of voices, a record of the "best" from 2015. An impossible task—there is no hierarchical or objective best—and only time, future readers, poets to come, will determine what is lasting. We no longer believe in the ancient literary ideal of "fame," which posits a posterity. And yet I found myself returning to certain poems and not others, sometimes for inexplicable reasons. It seems crucial to me to be open to different perspectives, a variety of poetic forms and experiments, a range of viewpoints, some of them having to do with class, gender, sexual orientation, ethnicity, and race. I am struck by how often these testimonials speak from a particular vantage point, from inside the experience of an "I," and present a witnessing. They will not be silenced. Whitman's empathic imagination remains a bedrock goal: "I do not ask the wounded person how he feels," he proclaims in "Song of Myself," "I myself become the wounded person."

I would go so far as to say that the lyric "I" is now returning with a vengeance. This book suggests that it is on the rise. The poets and theorists of the avant-garde, many of whom are white men, have consistently critiqued and disempowered the "I" in lyric poetry, the speaking subject. They have attacked the very idea of subject matter itself and displaced it with a theory of language as an entirely self-referential system. Poetry becomes free play. It courts meaninglessness. This critique of meaning in poetry, which initially came from right-wing modernists and later from left-wing postmodernists, has all the entitlements of an elite institution. Despite its protestations, it reinforces the reigning power structure. Why is it that the avant-garde is in denial about the antisemitism, homophobia, misogyny, and racism that powered so much of the modernist project? It has been ruinous for ordinary, overlooked, and otherwise dispossessed people. The idea that subject matter is naïve or somehow shameful further marginalizes already marginalized voices by rendering mute their experience.

The reclamation of the democratic "I" is an implicit critique of the critique about poetry. It advances against the "advance-guard" and recovers poetic territory that has been prematurely relinquished. The responsive or revitalized "I" is not naïve but encompassing. Some of our poets are working in modes that have pushed beyond the formulas of postmodernism. They blow open the old-fashioned idea of a unified self, while also retaining what poetry does best, which is to press down on the present moment, to pursue meaning out of experience. There is genuine suffering in the world, the suffering of actual people, and poetry addresses this suffering almost better than anything else. We are not passive but active subjects both of personal and social history. Experience does not come to us prepackaged. It demands our attention, our intervention. Losses accrue, memory is a responsibility. We have not entirely abandoned our posts. Some of our poets have decided to answer the call for a poetry of clarity and mystery.

This book is multitudinous. A number of these poets I've been reading for decades, others are entirely new to me. I made many discoveries—at least they were discoveries to me—and I am glad to introduce a group of tough-minded younger poets, who are bringing news from the front. There are at least three generations represented here. And I am grateful to be able to include six poets who are no longer alive—Frank Stanford, Larry Levis, Claudia Emerson, James Tate, C. K. Williams, and Philip Levine—but whose work continues to live. Charlie Williams and Phil Levine were two of my dearest friends and role models in poetry, and I especially mourn them.

Kenneth Burke calls literature "equipment for living." It is precisely that. Every couple of years someone comes along and enthusiastically pronounces that poetry is dead. It is not. On the contrary, it is an art form that continues to thrive in unexpected ways, engaging and evading its own history, setting out on unknown paths. We live, perhaps we have always lived, in perilous times, and stand on the edge of an abyss, which absorbs us. We are called to task. Poetry enlarges our experience. It brings us greater consciousness, fuller being. It stands on the side of life, our enthrallment.

THE
BEST
AMERICAN
POETRY
2016

CHRISTOPHER BAKKEN

Sentence

◇ ◇ ◇

No one predicted we'd be sitting there,
just come in from a blizzard to that bar,
and three beached fishermen in the corner
would interrupt their beans to stare at us,
then return to eating, since we were strange,
but cold enough to be left alone,
and that to expect their calm dismissal
of our being there showed we understood
how things worked then, in the dead decades,
after most of the city had vanished
on trains, or had been drowned in foreign ports;
and therefore, when the priest arrived
with his ice-crusted shawl and frozen cross,
crooning mangled hymns, his head gone to praise,
we'd think it right to offer him a seat,
would carry his stiff gloves to the fire,
and fill his glass with wine and pass him bread,
and would suffer the blessings he put
upon the empty wombs of our soup bowls;
and who knew we'd pretend to sing each verse
of the tune he'd use to condemn us,
but would have no answer to his slammed fist,
nor the thing he'd yell to be overheard
by everyone there—*when you stand this close
to the other side, don't embarrass yourselves
with hope*—as if that would be saying it all,
as if he knew we already stood there,

as if we could mount some kind of defense
before snow turned back to water in his beard.

from *Birmingham Poetry Review*

O Esperanza!

◊   ◊   ◊

Turns out my inner clown is full of hope.
She wants a gavel.
She wants to stencil her name on a wooden gavel:
Esperanza's Gavel.
Clowns are clichés and they aren't afraid of clichés.
Mine just sleeps when she's tired.
But she can't shake the hopes.
She's got a bad case of it, something congenital perhaps.
Maybe it was sexually transmitted,
something to do with oxytocin or contractions or nipple stimulation,
maybe that's it, a little goes a long way.
Hope is also the name of a bakery in Queens.
And there's a lake in Ohio called Hope Lake where you can get nachos.
I'm so stuffed with it the comedians in the Cellar never call on me,
even when I'm sitting right there in the front row with a dumb look of hope on
    my face.
Look at these books: hope.
Look at this face: hope.
When I was young I studied with Richard Rorty, that was lucky,
I stared out the window and couldn't understand a word he said,
he drew a long flat line after the C he gave me,
the class was called metaphysics and epistemology,
that's eleven syllables, that's
hope hope hope hope hope hope hope hope hope hope hope.
Just before he died, Rorty said his sense of the holy was bound up with the hope
that someday our remote descendants will live in a global civilization
in which love is pretty much the only law.

from *Tin House*

Whitman, 1841

◊   ◊   ◊

I don't know if he did or did not touch the boy.
But the boy told a brother or a father or a friend,
who told someone in a tavern, or told someone

about it while the men hauled in the nets of fish
from the Sound. Or maybe it was told to someone
on the street, a group of men talking outside

the village schoolhouse, where he was the teacher.
And what was said brought everyone to church
that Sunday, where the preacher said his name

from the pulpit and the pews cleared to find him.
He was twenty-one, thought of himself as an exile.
He was boarding with the boy and his family.

The boy was a boy in that schoolroom he hated.
Not finding him in the first house, they found him
in another and dragged him from under the bed

where he had been hiding. He was led outside.
And they took the tar they used for their boats,
and they broke some pillows for their feathers,

and the biography talks about those winter months
when there was not a trace of him, until the trail
of letters, articles, stories, and poems started

up again and showed he was back in the big city.
He was done with teaching. That was one part
of himself completed, though the self would never

be final, the way his one book of poems would
never stop taking everything into itself. The look
of the streets and the buildings. The look of men

and women. The names of ferry boats and trains.
The name of the village, which was Southold.
The name of the preacher, which was Smith.

from *Waxwing*

JILL BIALOSKY

Daylight Savings

◇   ◇   ◇

There was the hour
when raging with fever
they thrashed. The hour
when they called out in fright.
The hour when they fell asleep
against our bodies, the hour
when without us they might die.
The hour before school
and the hour after.
The hour when we buttered their toast
and made them meals
from the four important food groups—
what else could we do to ensure they'd get strong and grow?
There was the hour when we were spectators
at a recital, baseball game,
when they debuted in the school play.
There was the silent hour in the car
when they were angry. The hour
when they broke curfew. The hour
when we waited for the turn of the lock
knowing they were safe and we could finally
close our eyes and sleep. The hour
when they were hurt
or betrayed and there was nothing we could do
to ease the pain.
There was the hour
when we stood by their bedsides with ginger-ale
or juice until the fever broke. The hour
when we lost our temper and the hour

we were filled with regret. The hour
when we slapped their cheeks and held
our hand in wonder.
The hour when we wished for more.
The hour when their tall and strong bodies,
their newly formed curves and angles in their faces
and Adam's apple surprised us—
who had they become?
Hours when we waited and waited.
When we rushed home from the office
or sat in their teacher's classroom
awaiting the report of where they stumbled
and where they excelled, the hours
when they were without us, the precious hour
we did not want to lose each year
even if it meant another hour of daylight.

from *Harvard Review*

Fruits de Mer

◊   ◊   ◊

2011

A swirling blackness in the 20th, only the eyes visible,
or *Le Monde* on a historic morning, ink-heavy headline heaving
on the ground like a soldier who cannot stop the dark
from leaving his body. At Père Lachaise,
a coven of teenagers in black trench coats gathers,
like unfurled umbrellas, at Jim Morrison's grave,
there to light a candle to their idol's bones. A former America's
Sweetheart played his girlfriend in the biopic.
Shocking to see her on heroin, whining *Jim, Jim*, with beads in her
hair. Another image-makeover, and she's a slain Army
captain in Kabul, or was it Baghdad, or elsewhere? She kept at it
until youth left her, and now her face is ruined.
At Les Invalides, a taxidermied horse is the last sight
at the end of a corridor, a prize or cordial for enduring the war
placards. In cardinal red, the general is bemused, assured,
landing like a gangster bird anywhere he fancied.
Better an actual cardinal than more bloodshed.
Better a dove or a hawk, the predator caught on video attacking,
with talons, a drone, which seemed a victory for Nature.
This is the Age of Photographs, blown-up
Syrian children on the Pont des Arts where initialed locks
promise unbreakable love, keys scuttling through the Seine.
In flock-formation, helicopters arrive in Pakistan.
Bin Laden's dead, *Justice est faite*, served like something delicious.
Justice as a concept is both annealing and a terror. Let's go,
instead, to that place where Hemingway wrote and order
fruits de mer, its extravagant seduction, prelude to

buttery lovemaking. It's so outrageous, if we had to pay first
we'd never do it. But oh how the oyster trembles in the throat,
prawns like mistresses in the bed of a lobster king, bewitching him.
Towering rubble of mussels, the Belgians eat the rest by
using the first one's shell as a pincer. They held the Maginot Line
for three days before it was broken, becoming a historical joke.
Three days is nothing, a Memorial Day weekend, digging clams
at the seashore and laughing at how fast it goes.

from *Parnassus*

Ugglig

◇ ◇ ◇

Clock in the hall, tea in cups, Henry James
has come to call on George Eliot. "To begin with,"
he writes his father, "she is magnificently ugly,
deliciously hideous." James is twenty-six—
forgive him for flexing his wit as his pen
strides under a lamp burning with whale oil,
and let's go where ugly began, Old Norse,
Iceland riding a gash in the earth's crust
so that slow kisses burble the stinking mud
and hot goo geysers in hairy splendor.
Off-shore, the whale-roads are so thick
with monsters that were you nimble enough
you could dash across their breaching. Ugly,
ugglig, the choke and glub of drowning,
overcome outside your element
among the flowing families of swimmers
with faces not meant to be looked at.
Ugly is the mother of the sublime—dreadful
and magnetic, it sucks you over edges
with the torque of awe, so much like love
it must be love. "Now in this vast ugliness,"
James continues, "resides the most powerful
beauty which, in a very few minutes steals forth
and charms the mind, so you end as I ended,
in falling in love with her." And Eliot
in her horse-faced glory? All her life she's watched
faces recoil and collect, pulling down their shades.
Her eyes open farther and farther, terrorizing
with tenderness as she peers through the viscous

heat that ego sizzles in, the flaps of pride
and currents of loneliness nursed on dumb hurts.
She reaches in and grabs the beating soul.

from *The Gettysburg Review*

I Get to Float Invisible

◇   ◇   ◇

Someone's sister in Europe writing her
adultery poems late night, half bottle
of wine pretty much required.

And they're good, they really are—

The things one hears in an elevator.
Perfect strangers. I've always loved
the *perfect* part, as if news of the world is

a matter of pitch, and pure.

Maybe the desire of others only
simplifies me, seems generous that way.
It's the distance, an intimacy

so far from here I get to float invisible
all over, over again like I never
lived this life. What could be

lonelier, more full of

mute ringing than what
she's writing. That, and the wine.
Thus we pass the minutes,

ground to five, then six. And the door opens

because someone else pressed
the button first.
All along dark and light

take turns falling to earth.
And the sister
having sipped from a glass

and left behind such small shocks

is no doubt
asleep by now. I forget. Given
the time change.

from *The Georgia Review*

Hubert Blankenship

◇   ◇   ◇

Needing credit, he edges through the heavy door, head down,
and quietly closes the screen behind him.

This is Blankenship, father of five, owner of a plow horse and a cow.

Out of habit he leans against the counter by the stove.
He pats the pockets of his overalls

for the grocery list penciled on a torn paper bag,
then rolls into a strip of newsprint

the last of his Prince Albert.
He hardly takes his eyes off his boot, sliced on one side

to accommodate his bunion, and hands
the list to my grandfather. Bull of the Woods, three tins

of sardines, Spam, peanut butter, two loaves of bread (Colonial),
then back to the musty feed room

where he ignores the hand truck leaning against the wall

and hefts onto his shoulder a hundred-pound bag of horse feed.
He rises to full height, snorting

but hardly burdened,
and parades, head high, to the bed of his pickup.

from *The Southern Review*

32 Fantasy Football Teams

◇   ◇   ◇

1. The Grackles
2. The Receivers Not Taken
3. A Season in Hell
4. Love's Austere and Lonely Offensive Linemen
5. I Have Wasted My Draft Picks
6. The Zukofsky's A's
7. Because I could not stop for Penalties—
8. Letters to a Young Punter
9. The Center Cannot Block
10. The Newark Wastelands
11. [Bird Metaphor]
12. The Gloaming
13. I am large, I contain multiple playbooks
14. This Is Just to Sack
15. 13 Ways of Rushing Your Blindside
16. F=O=O=T=B=A=L=L
17. The End Zone Oath
18. La Fantasy Team Sans Merci
19. Iambic Puntameter
20. The Wildcards at Coole
21. Concussed, I is an other
22. Bengal Bengal, burning bright
23. my playing career did this to me
24. Leda and the Sweep
25. The Washington Hiawathas
26. First and Tender Buttons
27. The White Chickens
28. What Narcissism Means to Pacman Jones

from *32 Poems*

Last Morning
with Steve Orlen

◊ ◊ ◊

"Last night I wrote a Russian novel or maybe it was English.
Either way, it was long and boring. My wife's laughter
might tell you which it was, and when she stops,
when she's not laughing, let's talk about the plot,
and its many colors. The blue that hovered in the door
where the lovers held each other but didn't kiss.
The red that by mistake rose in the sky with the moon,
and the moon-colored sun that wouldn't leave the sky.
All night I kept writing it down, each word arranged
in my mouth, but now, as you can see, I'm flirting
with my wife. I'm making her laugh. She's twenty.
I'm twenty-five, just as we were when we met, just
as we have always been, except for last night's novel,
Russian or English, with its shimmering curtain of color,
an unfading show of Northern Lights, what you, you asshole,
might call *Aurora Borealis*.
So sit down on the bed with my wife and me.
Faithful amanuensis, you can write down my last words,
not that they're great but maybe they are.
You wouldn't know. You're an *Aurora Borealis*.
But my wife is laughing and you're laughing too.
Just as we were at the beginning, just as we are at the end."

from *The Greensboro Review* and *Poetry Daily*

ALLISON DAVIS

The Heart of It All
+ A Free Beer

◊   ◊   ◊

There are too many things set
    in Ohio. There is even a river. For a while
all we had were couches and tongue rings.
    Now, it's over. All married. Each time you turned around
to face the Torah I hoped you were looking
    at my ass. You weren't, and your brother wasn't looking
at my sister. We've recovered. She married.
    In Youngstown when you marry there's a cookie table.
Back home, having a long last name
    is like having a big dick, is like having a nice
cookie table. My five aunts made hundreds
    of Greek cookies for my sister's wedding.
My mother would make them for school, at Christmas,
    and I'd bring them in with her motherly note:
"Take out the clove! xo" After my sister's wedding,
    my mother packed up a box of cookies
and said, "Don't share them with anyone
    who won't appreciate them." My mother's nightmare
is someone eating Greek food without having
    an experience. Baklava is something she has left
of one experience. My cousin
    cries about a guy, and I say, "Good, no one likes him
anyway." No, I don't. I say, "Find someone
    who'll treat it like an experience." And if you do
and if he doesn't, forget about the clove.
    He'll ask, "Was I supposed to swallow that?"

Answer, "That's what she said." My cousin
        rolls her eyes, says I don't
understand. The time spent convincing the heartbroken
        you've been heartbroken. The last time I saw him
was in a Columbus library. We'd both left town,
        yet there we were: the back of his neck
in Literature, D-F. "I could not speak, and my eyes failed,
        I was neither living nor dead" are *Waste Land* lines
Pound wasn't allowed to cut. A hallucination?
        I emailed: it was him, he asked why I didn't say
hello. Because it's possible to stay too long
        at the fair. Because aisles over in L
was the Lorca
        I once watched a guy from Madrid
angrily re-translate in red ink. Even now, it's there—
        written and written
over. Even now, a Great Lake
        and a river. Things are set in Ohio
because you're allowed to stay too long
        and call it love. Because there are no
regulations. My mother waits up
        for my father who works at a motel
that never closes, that gives customers
        the heart of whatever they've come for
plus a free beer with every room.

                from *Sycamore Review*

On the Certainty of Bryan

◇ ◇ ◇

Bryan is ~~very~~ certain about the Ocean Park paintings of Richard Diebenkorn.
~~They are very good.~~
He does not have to say (or see) much more.
He especially likes the ~~almost~~ empty light blue one that is like an iceberg.
He also likes dense black-and-white photography, Japanese.
Not a soul, empty are the streets and houses he looks at/makes.
Yet people (have) live(d) there.
I guess I can see what he is not talking about (we can both smell Lyana's
       ~~super~~ stinkyfeet), but I would be unsure or even left out without the
       certainty of Bryan. Bryan, should we have a drink? <Sure.>
Back in Alaska, I have opened the window to/on spring. New ideas are breezing
       in, like students. I am: like students.

Did you read Eileen Myles's interview in that issue with the tongue
through/on the front? Despite my original skepticism, did she soothe me,
if only for a moment? I am completely unclear
on: my skepticism, ways, talents, dollars, "integrity," days, art(s). My life, it felt
       hard, hard, hard, hard, a little easier, fucking unbearable, hard, but was it?

Someone pretty smart was crying.
I did not know what to do.
"Now I'm tired and confused," I said, unable to tell what was going on
in someone (another someone) else's loins.
Then, once or twice, scared all afternoon of something that ended up
tasting: like baby food. Bryan has a big house in Brooklyn, a big job downtown,
       a small child, a wife. His daughter goes to this little school in a
       basement in Chinatown. Eileen Myles might have passed them a year
       or two ago, on the way to fake beg.

Maybe if this was a short story the poignancy would hover in a short story
        atrium-y area,
maybe at the daycare/school and descend like light
on a certain mother or "wife." She is now a few blocks away, catching
her own reflection in that worn warm mitt.
But why should I introduce any more characters?
We have Bryan, we have Diebenkorn, Myles, <the Japanese,> Bryan's kid and
        Bryan's wife. "We" have "me." Isn't that poignant enough?

There are mothers at the school and there are motherlikebutyounger teachers, but
        so far they all look the same. Yes, they have sick problems, but: This is
        not by Sam Lipsyte!

Oh, shit, Lydia Davis, yes, sure, if it's you, come in. Come in. Translate
        something from Dutch. And BTW WTF did you learn to speak/translate
        from Dutch?

I always am afraid to say "Dutch" and "the Netherlands";
never "Holland"; rarely "de Kooning," and is that d fucking capital or what?
"One lip, tulips" and then they both laughed on my back deck cause
they liked each other so it was funny and of absolutely no interest to me, except
        here it is. somehow. again.

I have spent a month thinking about Bryan and his absolute certainty about certain
        paintings and photographs and how he matter-of-factly but quietly
        admitted that this certainty did not translate to his work. his life.
Do I know what I like
even a little?

I keep looking at the Diebenkorns online, maybe
wanting the book, which if I got I would forget to look at.
Supposedly he flew over a lot of stuff and liked how that looked.
Empty was the earth below, yet full of lots of people, no?

So I said/asked: "Bryan, I am thinking maybe of writing a poem
about your certainty. What was the title of that Diebenkorn that made you start to
        draw icebergs?"

Bryan says he will look it up after he gets home from work. He says:
"I hope it has a happy ending."

"Oh, that was John Zurier's 'The Future of Ice.' Never heard of him," he says,
    absolutely unshaken.

Is there shit under my fingernail?
Is this meat I am feeding my children tainted?
When is the last time I had sex?

Meanwhile, Kary and I discuss the new *New Yorker* poem by Louise Glück.
She says: "I was waiting for you to love it to love it." and "I like how she rhymed
    'precipice' with 'pillowcase.'"
"I didn't notice (pang), but
I liked the relief tainted by the need to respond and I have also been meaning to
    say/ask:

that one The Cave Singers song about getting younger? and
are you still flirting with Peter Richards online, cause:
'After a while I came to know that death was the hay . . .'"

Then, out of the blue, out of a southeast Alaskan clear blue-green pit,
actually, Dylan comes to visit, like some
traveling salesman of complexity. Jesus, he was
raised on a commune in Florida, he remembers the six buildings, the main dude
    who was some gay doctor, the way they had to sit and watch things
    burn, and he can see things before they happen
but what is happening that isn't, that brings him here looking for a friend in
patient and kind yet so unwilling "me"?
patient and kind yet so unwilling, "I"
meant everything, my seventy-two hours of statements,

but:
so?

Back to nothing.
Suicidal panic.
I am broke and I am old.

Or I am still pretty
young and are these riches,
or fucking what?

and:

What did you think
of the poem with the mouse in it?
What did you think of the mouse?

from *Alaska Quarterly Review*

How the Milky Way Was Made

◊   ◊   ◊

My river was once unseparated. Was Colorado. Red-
fast flood. Able to take

       anything it could wet—in a wild rush—

       all the way to Mexico.

Now it is shattered by fifteen dams
over one-thousand-four-hundred-and-fifty miles,

pipes and pumps filling
swimming pools and sprinklers

       in Los Angeles and Las Vegas.

To save our fish, we lifted them from our skeletoned riverbeds,
loosed them in our heavens, set them aster—
       'Achii 'ahan, Mojave salmon,

       Colorado pikeminnow—

Up there they glide gilled with stars.
You see them now—

       god-large, gold-green sides,

       moon-white belly to breast—

making their great speeded way across the darkest hours,
rippling the sapphired sky-water into a galaxy road.

The blurred wake they drag as they make their path
through the night sky is called

       'Achii 'ahan nyuunye—

              our words for *Milky Way*.

Coyote too is up there, locked in the moon
after his failed attempt to leap it, fishing net wet

       and empty slung over his back—

              a prisoner blue and dreaming

of unzipping the salmon's silked skins with his teeth.
O, the weakness of any mouth

       as it gives itself away to the universe

              of a sweet-milk body.

Just as my own mouth is dreamed to thirst
the long desire-ways, the hundred-thousand-light-year roads

       of your wrists and thighs.

        from *American Poets*

Humanity 101

◇   ◇   ◇

I was on my way to becoming a philanthropist,
or the president, or at least someone who gave a shit,
but I was a nontraditional student
with a lot of catching up to do. I enrolled in Humanity 101
(not to be confused with the Humanities,
a whole separate department). When I flunked
the final exam, my professor suggested
I take Remedial Humanity where I'd learn the basics
that I'd missed so far. I may have been a nontraditional student
but I was a traditional person, she said, the way a professor
can say intimate things sometimes, as though
your face and soul are aglow in one of those
magnified (✕ 10) makeup mirrors.

So I took Remedial Humanity, which sounds like an easy A,
but, believe me, it was actually quite challenging.
There were analogy questions such as:
Paris Hilton is to a rich U.S. suburban kid
as a U.S. middle-class kid is to:
1. a U.S. poverty-stricken kid
2. a U.S. kid with nothing in the fridge
or
3. a Third World kid with no fridge at all.
We were required to write essays about the cause of war—
Was it a phenomenon? Was it our lower animal selves?
Was it economics? Was it psychological/sexual/religious
(good vs. evil and all that stuff)? For homework
we had to bend down to talk to a homeless person
slouched against a building. We didn't necessarily have to

give them money or food, but we had to say something like
How are you? or *What is your favorite color?*

We took field trips to nursing homes, prisons,
daycare centers. We stood near bedsides
or sat on the floor to color with strange little people
who cried and were afraid of us at first.
I almost dropped out. I went to see the professor
during his office hours because I wanted to change my major.
He asked, "Is that because your heart is being smashed?"
He thought I should stick it out, that I could make it,
if I just escaped for an hour a day blasting music
from my earbuds or slumping in front of the TV.
I said, "But that's just it. Now I see humanity everywhere,
even on sitcoms, even in pop songs,
even in beer commercials." He closed his door
and showed me the scars under his shirt
where he had been stabbed. He said I had to assume
everyone had such a wound, whether I could see it or not.

He assured me that it really did get easier in time,
and that it was hard to break the rules until you knew
how to play the scale. He made me see
my potential. He convinced me of my own humanity,
that one day I might even be able to get a PhD. But first
I had to write, for extra credit, a treatise on detachment.

from *The Southern Review*

My Life

◇　◇　◇

Like Jonas by the fish was I received by it,
swung and swept in its dark waters,
driven to the deeps by it and beyond many rocks.
Without any touching of its teeth, I tumbled into it
with no more struggle than a mote of dust
entering the door of a cathedral, so muckle were its jaws.
How heel over head was I hurled down
the broad road of its throat, stopped inside
its chest wide as a hall, and like Jonas I stood up
asking where the beast was and finding it nowhere,
there in grease and sorrow I build my bower.

from *The New York Times Magazine*

Cyst

◊   ◊   ◊

She had once had an abortion, she said, and later
an affair with a married man,

then another, her solitude always
uneasy, her body

lonely for something nameless as they had been,
or as she made them.

She said it began as pressure not quite pain,
and they found it outside

the womb, clinging to an ovary, having
conceived of itself.

When they removed it, they told her she could see it
if she wanted to:

just a curiosity with teeth, hair, and nails. Odd
but benign, the doctor

said, most always benign, nodding toward it
as though it could agree

with him, as though that were the fact,
the whole of it: curious

mistake a body can make.

from *Subtropics*

MARTÍN ESPADA

Here I Am

◊　◊　◊

for José "JoeGo" Gouveia (1964–2014)

He swaggered into the room, a poet at a gathering of poets,
and the drinkers stopped crowding the cash bar, the talkers stopped
their tongues, the music stopped hammering the walls, the way
a saloon falls silent when a gunslinger knocks open the swinging doors:
JoeGo grinning in gray stubble and wraparound shades, leather Harley
vest, shirt yellow as a prospector's hallucination, sleeve buttoned
to hide the bandage on his arm where the IV pumped chemo through
his body a few hours ago. The nurse swabbed the puncture and told him
he could go, and JoeGo would go, gunning his red van from the Cape
to Boston, striding past the cops who guarded the hallways of the grand
convention center, as if to say *Here I am*: the butcher's son, the Portagee,
the roofer, the carpenter, the cab driver, the biker-poet. This was JoeGo,
who would shout his ode to Evel Knievel in biker bars till the brawlers
rolled in beer and broken glass, who married Josy from Brazil
on the beach after the oncologist told him he had two months to live
two years ago. *That's not enough for me*, he said, and will say again
when the cancer comes back to coil around his belly and squeeze hard
like a python set free and starving in the swamp. He calls me on his cell
from the hospital, and I can hear him scream when they press the cold
X-ray plates to his belly, but he will not drop the phone. He wants
the surgery today, right now, surrounded by doctors with hands
blood-speckled like the hands of his father the butcher, sawing
through the meat for the family feast. The patient's chart should read:
This is JoeGo: after every crucifixion, he snaps the cross across his back
for firewood. He will roll the stone from the mouth of his tomb and bowl
a strike. On the night he silenced the drinkers chewing ice in my ear,

a voice in my ear said: *What the hell is that man doing here?*
And I said: *That man there? That man will live forever.*

from *The American Poetry Review*

The Kiskiminetas River

◇   ◇   ◇

It begins in the seepage of salt wells,
as if waking from a dream of the sea
before it gathers itself and runs

for twenty-seven restless, hardworking
miles, only to lose itself, swept inland
toward Pittsburgh and the vast Ohio Valley.

Kiskiminetas: the Lenape name means
clear stream of many bends or *break camp*,
the etymology unclear but apt:

whenever the Lenape tried to settle,
someone came along and moved them
to a place no one wanted.

My grandfather, in Italy a farmer, dug coal
not far from where it empties into the Allegheny.
His sons would inherit and divide his labor:

coal mines, steel mills, foundries.
The river turned sulfur-orange and stank
from all the mines draining into it—

nothing could live in its waters.
Even the stones of the riverbed took on
the petrified figures of the lost:

Shy Charlie, who took a header off the bridge;
Bobby, who slipped into the current
like raw sewage; my father, who flew

his car over its cindered embankment
in the hard winter of my birth.
Nothing is held in place by a name;

the river changes and is ever changeless.
Today, the mines are closed; the small towns
seem emptier and forlorn at night;

the river runs clear, its surface
shifting in the slant of morning light
or the passing shadows of its seasons.

On the bluffs, overlooking the valley,
my grandfather and his sons have come to rest
among the now, or soon to be, forgotten.

from *The Southern Review*

When I turned fourteen, my mother's sister took me to lunch and said:

◊   ◊   ◊

soon you'll have breasts. They'll mushroom on your
smooth chest like land mines.

A boy will show up, a schoolmate, or the gardener's son.
Pole-cat around you. All brown-eyed persistence.

He'll be everything your parents hate, a smart aleck,
a dropout, a street racer on the midnight prowl.

Even your best friend will call him a loser.
But this boy will steal your reason, have you

writing his name inside a scarlet heart, entwined
with misplaced passion and a bungled first kiss.

He'll bivouac beneath your window, sweet-talk you
until you sneak out into his waiting complications.

Go ahead, tempt him with your new-found glamour.
Tumble into the backseat of his Ford at the top of Mulholland,

flushed with stardust, his mouth in a death-clamp on your nipple,
his worshipful fingers scatting sacraments on your clit.

Soon he will deceive you with your younger sister,
the girl who once loved you most in the world.

from *Ragazine*

One Had Lived in a Room
and Loved Nothing

◊   ◊   ◊

One had lived in a room and loved nothing.
Full of spiders and what memory remained,
one had loved and she had forgotten things.

Clock stopped and aeroplane lost in the dark,
and who was that voice on the telephone?
One had lived in a room and loved nothing.

It was a rare sleep in helter-skelter;
one awakened a half-blessed and charmed fool.
One had loved and she had forgotten things.

One had lived in a room and loved nothing
left alone in her wedding gown and throne.
Who gave her a mantis kiss as jazz played?

The faceless lover and last known address,
a writing pad and table overturned,
one had loved and she had forgotten things.

What was day or night with no hours left
and who were the two in the photograph?
One had loved and she had forgotten things.
One had lived in a room and loved nothing.

from *Green Mountains Review*

EMILY FRAGOS

The Sadness of Clothes

◇ ◇ ◇

When someone dies, the clothes are so sad. They have outlived
their usefulness and cannot get warm and full.
You talk to the clothes and explain that he is not coming back

as when he showed up immaculately dressed in slacks and plaid jacket
and had that beautiful smile on and you'd talk.
You'd go to get something and come back and he'd be gone.

You explain death to the clothes like that dream.
You tell them how much you miss the spouse
and how much you miss the pet with its little winter sweater.

You tell the worn raincoat that if you talk about it,
you will finally let grief out. The ancients etched the words
for battle and victory onto their shields and then they went out

and fought to the last breath. Words have that kind of power
you remind the clothes that remain in the drawer, arms stubbornly
folded across the chest, or slung across the backs of chairs,

or hanging inside the dark closet. Do with us what you will,
they faintly sigh, as you close the door on them.
He is gone and no one can tell us where.

from Poem-a-Day

AMY GERSTLER

A Drop of Seawater
Under the Microscope

◇ ◇ ◇

Who knew this little bit of spillage
contained multitudes of what we all

boil down to? Microorganisms
swim a surface the wet silver

of Poseidon's eyes. Spiralized lines,
pulsing globules, tiny sacs filled with aspic.

Obscenely, you can see right through
them, sometimes down to their nuclei.

They come in lovely colors.
Is this natural or has the scientist

who slid their slide under the microscope
stained them orange, ochre and blue

for better viewing? Their outlines
waver like hand-drawn cartoons.

They resemble party favors,
tiny offspring of a bubble cluster

and the plankton alphabet.
Why, then, have I been so afraid

of what I am made of breaking down
into constituent parts, of one day

rejoining this infinitesimal assembly,
of becoming an orgy of particles

too (beautiful and) numerous to count?

from *Valley Voices*

DANA GIOIA

Meet Me at the Lighthouse

◇　◇　◇

Meet me at the Lighthouse in Hermosa Beach,
That shabby nightclub on its foggy pier.
Let's aim for the summer of '71,
When all of our friends were young and immortal.

I'll pick up the cover charge, find us a table,
And order a round of their watery drinks.
Let's savor the smoke of that sinister century,
Perfume of tobacco in the tangy salt air.

The crowd will be quiet—only ghosts at the bar—
So you, old friend, won't feel out of place.
You need a night out from that dim subdivision.
Tell Mr. Bones you'll be back before dawn.

The club has booked the best talent in Tartarus.
Gerry, Cannonball, Hampton, and Stan,
With Chet and Art, those gorgeous greenhorns—
The swinging-masters of our West Coast soul.

Let the All-Stars shine from that jerry-built stage.
Let their high notes shimmer above the cold waves.
Time and the tide are counting the beats.
Death the collector is keeping the tab.

from *Virginia Quarterly Review*

Reading to My Father

◇   ◇   ◇

I come back indoors at dusk-end. I come back into the room with

your now finished no-longer-aching no-longer-being

body in it, the candle beside you still lit—no other

light for now. I sit by it and look at it. Another *in*

from the one I was just peering-out towards now, over

rooftops, over the woods, first stars.

The candle burns. It is so quiet you can hear it burn.

Only I breathe. I hear that too.

Listen I say to you, forgetting. Do you hear it Dad. Listen.

What is increase. The cease of increase.

The cease of progress. What is progress.

What is going. The cease of going.

What is knowing. What is fruition.

The cease of. Cease of.

What is bloodflow. The cease of bloodflow

of increase of progress the best is over, is over-

thrown, no, the worst is yet to come, no, it is

7:58 pm, it is late spring, it is capital's apogee, the

flow's, fruition's, going's, increase's, in creases of

matter, brainfold, cellflow, knowing's

pastime, it misfired, lifetime's only airtime—candle says

you shall *out* yourself, out-

perform yourself, grow multiform—you shall self-identify as

                                                still

mortal—here in this timestorm—this end-of-time

storm—the night comes on.

Last night came on with you still *here*.

Now I wait here. Feel *I can think*. Feel *there are no minutes in you*—

Put my minutes there, on you, as hands—touch, press,

feel the flying-away, the leaving-sticks-behind under the skin, then even the skin

abandoned now, no otherwise now, even the otherwise gone.

I lay our open book on you, where we left off. I read. I read aloud—

grove, forest, jungle, dog—the words don't grip-up into sentences for me,

                         it is in pieces,

I start again into the space above you—*grandeur wisdom village,*

tongue, street, wind—hornet—feeler runner rust red more—oh

more—I hear my voice—it is so raised—on you—are you—*refinery portal*

land scald difference—here comes my *you*, rising in me, my feel-

                              ing your *it*, my *me*, increasing, elaborating, flowing, not yet released from form, not yet,

still will-formed, swarming, mis-

informed—*bridegroom of spume and vroom.*

I touch your pillowcase. I read this out to you as, in extremis, we await

those who will come to fix you—make you permanent. No more vein-hiss. A

                                        masterpiece. My phantom

father-body—so gone—how gone. I sit. Your suit laid out. Your silver tie. Your

                                        shirt. I don't know

                                        what is

needed now. It's day. *Read now*, you'd say. Here it is then, one last time, the

                                        news. I

                                        read. *There is no*

precedent for, far exceeds the ability of, will not

                                        adapt to, cannot

                                        adapt to,

but not for a while yet, not yet, but not for much longer, no, much

sooner than predicted, yes, ten times, a hundred times, all evidence

                                        points towards.

                                        What do I tell my child.

Day has arrived and crosses out the candle-light. Here it is now the

silent summer—extinction—migration—the blue-jewel-

butterfly you loved, goodbye, the red kite, the dunnock, the crested tit, the cross-

billed spotless starling (near the top of the list) smokey gopher—spud-wasp—the named storms, extinct fonts, ingots, blindmole-made-

tunnels—oh your century, there in you, how it goes out—

how lonely are we aiming for—are we there

yet—the orange-bellied and golden-shouldered parrots—

I read them out into our room, I feel my fingers grip this

page, where are the men who are supposed to come for you,

most of the ecosystem's services, it says,

will easily become replaced—the soil, the roots, the webs—the organizations

of—the 3D grasses, minnows, mudflats—the virtual carapace—the simulated action of

forest, wetland, of all the living noise that keeps us

company. Company. I look at you.

Must I be this machine I am

become. This brain programming

blood function, flowing beating releasing channeling.

This one where I hold my head in my hands and the chip

slips in and *click* I go to find my in-

formation. The two-headed eagle, the

beaked snake, the feathered men walking sideways while looking

ahead, on stone, on wall, on pyramid, in

sacrifice—must I have already *become* when it is all still

happening. Behind you thin machines that ticked and hummed until just now

are off *for good.* What I wouldn't give, you had said last night, for five more

minutes here. *You can't imagine it.* Minutes ago.

Ago. It hums. It checks us now, monitoring

this minute fraction of—the MRI, the access-zone, the

aura, slot, logo, confession-

al—I feel the hissing multiplying

satellites out there I took for stars, the bedspread's weave, your *being* tucked-in—

goodnight, goodnight—*Once upon a time* I say into my air,

and I caress you now with the same touch

as I caress these keys.

from *Boston Review*

The Lady Responds

◇　◇　◇

after Sir Thomas Wyatt

Whoso list to hunt will need a hound,
a dog to lead the horses, chase the hare
and hind, dig the foxes from their lair.
How pretty their paws, tearing up the ground,
their white and crimson jaws when the prize is found!
But a mistress of hounds must take special care
not to treat one as a pet, to share
a morsel from her plate or let one bound
onto her bed. A dog must know its place,
at the mistress's feet rather than her lap.
A beast who misbehaves deserves a rap
across his nose, a kick till he's abased.
A cur that won't be muzzled or made to sit
must bait the unchained bears in the fighting pit.

from *River Styx*

Font

◊   ◊   ◊

At the foot of the download anchored
                              among
                    the usual flotsam of ads,

this link: to plastics-express.com who for
                              a fraction
                    of the retail price can

solve my underground drainage woes, which
                              tells me
                    the software has finally

run amok. Because the article, you see,
                              recounts
                    the rescue from a sewage

pipe of Baby 59, five pounds,
                              placenta still
                    attached, in Zhejiang

Province, where officials even as I read
                              are debating
                    the merits of throwing

the mother in jail. Communal
                              toilet. Father
                    nowhere to be found.

The gods in their mercy once
                              could turn
                    a frightened girl to

water or a shamed one to a tree,
                              but they
                    no longer seem

to take our troubles much
                              to heart.
                    And so the men with

hacksaws do their gentle best—consider
                    the infant
                    shoulders, consider the lids—

and this one child among millions,
                    delivered
                    a second time to what

we still call breathable air, survives
                    to pull
                    the cords of sentiment

and commerce.
                              Don't make the poem
                    too sad, says Megan,

thinking at first (we both of us
                              think) the child
                    must be a girl or otherwise

damaged, thus (this part she doesn't
                    say) like her.
                    Who is the ground

of all I hope and fear for in the world.
                              Who'll buy?
                    Or as the hawkers

on the pavement used to put it, What
                              d'you lack?
                    The download comes with

pictures too. Of workmen, wrenches,
                              bits of shattered
                    PVC, and one for whom

the whole of it—commotion, cameras,
                              IV needle in the scalp—
                    is not more strange

than ordinary daylight.
                              Welcome, Number
                    59. Here's milk

from a bottle and here's a nearly

                    human hand.

from *Raritan*

JENNIFER GROTZ

Self-Portrait on the Street of an Unnamed Foreign City

◊   ◊   ◊

The lettering on the shop window in which
you catch a glimpse of yourself is in Polish.

Behind you a man quickly walks by, nearly shouting
into his cell phone. Then a woman

at a dreamier pace, carrying a just-bought bouquet
upside-down. All on a street where pickpockets abound

along with the ubiquitous smell of something baking.
It is delicious to be anonymous on a foreign city street.

Who knew this could be a life, having languages
instead of relationships, struggling even then,

finding out what it means to be a woman
by watching the faces of men passing by.

I went to distant cities, it almost didn't matter
which, so primed was I to be reverent.

All of them have the beautiful bridge
crossing a gray, near-sighted river,

one that massages the eyes, focuses
the swooping birds that skim the water's surface.

The usual things I didn't pine for earlier
because I didn't know I wouldn't have them.

I spent so much time alone, when I actually turned lonely
it was vertigo.

Myself estranged is how I understood the world.
My ignorance had saved me, my vices fueled me,

and then I turned forty. I who love to look and look
couldn't see what others did.

Now I think about currencies, linguistic equivalents, how lopsided they are,
while my reflection blurs in the shop windows.

Wanting to be as far away as possible exactly as much as still with you.
Shamelessly entering a Starbucks (free wifi) to write this.

from Poem-a-Day

Doctor Scheef

◇   ◇   ◇

Doctor Scheef you probably tried hard
in 1971 at your clinic in Bonn
I assume you tried hard to save my mother
with your regime of enzyme injections
and 30 million units of Vitamin A

but you did not save my mother—
at best you gave her a little hope for a while
though I suspect she was too skeptical even for that
though she tried to believe for my father's sake;

Doctor Scheef you needed to be a historic genius
but you were not!
                              And so my mother went on hurting
month after month with cancer in her vertebrae and her spine
and she died after three more years of hurting
since you were not a historic genius Doctor Scheef
—and you must be dead by now too
and forgiving you would make sense no doubt
but I'm not ready, maybe I am not yet tired enough
so I prefer to name you here sternly

rather than settle for the letting go in forgiveness
as I am still in the non-genius condition of wanting
targets for complaint therefore I say that in 1971
you should have been a hell of a lot smarter Doctor Scheef.

from *Copper Nickel*

JEFFREY HARRISON

Afterword

◊   ◊   ◊

The maple limb severed
by a December storm
still blossoms in May
where it lies on the ground,

its red tassels a message
from the other side,
like a letter arriving
after its writer has died.

from *The New York Times Magazine*

Barberism

◇   ◇   ◇

It was light and lusterless and somehow luckless,
The hair I cut from the head of my father-in-law,

It was pepper-blanched and wind-scuffed, thin
As a blown bulb's filament, it stuck to the teeth

Of my clippers like a dark language, the static
Covering his mind stuck to my fingers, it mingled

In halfhearted tufts with the dust. Because
Every barber's got a gift for mind reading in his touch,

I could hear what he would not say. He'd sworn
To never let his hair be cut again after his daughter

Passed away. I told him how my own boy,
His grandchild, weeps when my clippers bite

Behind his ear, but I could not say how
The blood there tastes. I almost showed him

How I bow my own head to the razor in my hands,
How a mirror is used to taper the nape.

Science and religion come to the same conclusion:
Someday all the hair on the body will fall away.

I'm certain he will only call on me for a few more years,
The crown of his head is already smoother

Than any part of his face. It shines like the light
In tiny bulbs of sweat before the sweat evaporates.

from *The New York Times Magazine*

Bible Study

◇   ◇   ◇

Who would have imagined that I would have to go
a million miles away from the place where I was born
to find people who would love me?
And that I would go that distance and that I would find those people?

In the dream JoAnne was showing me how much arm to amputate
if your hand gets trapped in the machine;
if you act fast, she said, you can save everything above the wrist.
You want to keep a really sharp blade close by, she said.

Now I raise that hand to scratch one of those nasty little
scabs on the back of my head, and we sit outside and watch
the sun go down, inflamed as an appendicitis
over western Illinois—which then subsides and cools into a smooth gray wash.

Who knows, this might be the last good night of summer.
My broken nose is forming an idea of what's for supper.
Hard to believe that death is just around the corner.
What kind of idiot would think he even had a destiny?

I was on the road for so long by myself,
I took to reading motel Bibles just for company.
Lying on the chintz bedspread before going to sleep,
still feeling the motion of the car inside my body,
I thought some wrongness in my self had left me that alone.

And God said, *You are worth more to me*
than one hundred sparrows.

And when I read that, I wept.
And God said, *Whom have I blessed more than I have blessed you?*

And I looked at the minibar
and the bad abstract hotel art on the wall
and the dark TV set watching like a deacon.
And God said, *Survive. And carry my perfume among the perishing.*

from *Poetry*

The Unwritten Volume

◊   ◊   ◊

In memory of L.W.

from *In June, the Labyrinth*

*[The] narrative is genealogical but it does not simply amount to an
act of memory. It witnesses, in the manner of an ethical or politi-
cal act, for today and for tomorrow.*
                                    Jacques Derrida, *The Gift of Death*

Elle's writing her book of wisdom.
She writes until she cannot hold her pen.
The labyrinth miraculously is uncovered.

An American woman's progressing on her knees.
She read something but not Elle's book.
No one will read Elle's book.

I walk the circular path, first the left side,
then the right, casting petals to the north,
east, south, and west (this intuitively).

A diminutive prelate shoos me away.
When he leaves, I return to the center.
The organist, practicing, strikes up *Phantom*.

Elle says she cannot hear him.
Elle! I cry, *I cannot see you.*
I had prayed Death spare you.

Remember our meal among the termites
of Arcadia Street, that cottage of spirits
with its riddled beams and long veranda

bordered by plantain trees, and the spiral
you traced for me on scrap-paper?
I kept it for such a long time.

The organist, of course, is playing Bach.
A boy scattered the rose petals I cast
all over. Elle's voice surrounds me.

To quiet hills I lift mine eyes.

from *Prairie Schooner*

I Got Heaven . . .

◊　◊　◊

I swear that, in Gardena, on a moonlit suburban street,
There are souls that twirl like kites lashed to the wrists of the living
And spirits who tumble in a solemn limbo between 164th
And the long river of stars to Amida's Paradise in the West.

As though I belonged, I've come from my life of papers and exile
To walk among these penitents at the Festival of the Dead,
The booths full of sellers hawking rice cakes and candied plums,
All around us the rhythmic chant of *min'yō* bursting through
　　　　　loudspeakers,
Calling out the mimes and changes to all who dance.

I stop at a booth and watch a man, deeply tanned from work outdoors,
Pitch bright, fresh quarters into blue plastic bowls.
He wins a porcelain cat, a fishnet bag of marbles,
Then a bottle of *shōyu*, and a rattle shaped like tam-tam he gives to a child.

I hear the words of a Motown tune carry through the gaudy air
. . . got sunshine on a cloudy day . . . got the month of May . . .
As he turns from the booth and reenters the River of Heaven—
These dancers winding in brocades and silk sleeves,
A faith-lit circle briefly aswarm in the summer night.

from *Miramar*

Girls

◇ ◇ ◇

The point not that so-called ugly girls
get laid on HBO, but their mishaps, that if
the single one is funny, a slew of them looks

downright ambitious. They're the bitches
nobody liked in high school, smudge-eyed
and trussed up in complicated skirts,

queuing outside the club with their amber
vials of blow. Our kind of fucking up is Y,
less Millennial, more perpetual, because

we too called ourselves journalists,
wrote for weeklies nobody read. We too
got swept into green rooms on a glance,

our stupid luck that a drummer sized up
my platinum, six-foot, Australian friend
and invited us backstage. Instead, she ended up

with the frontman singing to her outside,
as the drummer droned on about offbeats
to me, his dark foil whinging about desire,

thinking, maybe, *she's a little bit fat.*
Even before he pushed a shrink-wrapped
CD like bus fare into my palm, I knew

our hook-up wouldn't do me any good—
my nights were transcendent in their flaws.
Earlier, when my friend pulled him off me,

her *what were you thinking* draped between us
like garlands at an anti-award ceremony,
I wanted to be a woman who could Take Back

Some Night Somewhere, hang with those bad
bitches at Seneca Falls. But I kissed a drummer
from Staten Island because he wanted

to kiss me. Does it get any less complicated
than one passed-over object burying itself
in another? To those who would say *Girls*

is the third wave finding itself, who speak
from the absurd position of having been *found*,
I offer this grounded but ahistorical Fuck You,

I swear our girlish centers burn white-hot
as surely as nothing burns there. It was last call
five minutes ago. Somebody, turn up the lights.

from *Crab Orchard Review*

85 Off & On

◊   ◊   ◊

"When, my dears, is the right age to die?"
Our hostess, the centenarian
Dorothea Tanning, saw herself
out of the running, but enjoyed
hounding her guests (and herself)
with this mean stickler—it was as if
one of the Fates was questioning us:

"David Alexander, I think you're
the youngest artist at this table:
how old would *you* decide one must be
to claim a Deathbed of Distinction?"
"*Ninety?*" David's scared digits seemed to
please Dorothea and the others . . .
Everyone but me. Count up the facts:

for the last sixty years of my life
I've attempted to do what I could
by way of poems, but it appears
that an alarming proportion of
Contemporary American Poets,
whose lives and works I believe I shared
in poetic and in social terms,

were having none of it: their lives ended!
Ammons   Wright   Plath   Warren   Bishop   Rich
Roethke   Clampitt   Van Doren   Van Duyn
Ginsberg   Rukeyser   Dugan   Lowell
Finkel   Simpson   Hollander   Merrill

Justice Nemerov Creeley Hugo
Hecht O'Hara Kizer Kunitz Koch

Ransom Moss Kinnell (and this week!) Strand.
It would be all too easy to fill
more of my stanzas with more of such
mortalities . . . Count them for yourself:
every one is dead. *And I'm alive!*
I know, I know: I can always *read*
them, but they can't read themselves (or me).

You see? Doing *anything*, even
writing poems, is something
we all must be alive for—only
we're not all alive. *Not all alive* . . .
Which is why we write, why I must write
this poem right now, this time around
at a mere eighty-five. Certainly

I didn't know them all—the dead ones—
intimately. Some of those I loved
most (read most often) I never knew
really well. But once he or she died
I discovered that, as Tolstoy says,
they'd been the most precious, the dearest,
and most necessary of beings.

It's unlikely I (or anyone)
will be celebrating his or her
ninety-fifth birthday. Or would even
want to. That's why it occurred to me
—for reasons designated above—
this is the proper occasion to write
my eighty-fifth birthday poem now.

from *The Yale Review*

Minutiae

◊   ◊   ◊

I never underestimate the housefly, its micro-mechanism
   buzzed with vinegar and honey, its hairy guts
Splattered on the kitchen window. I pay homage likewise
   to the spider and the wood louse, the emperor moth
And the wasp. All these souls precede us. Where would I be
   without the carpenter ant and the exalted one, the scarab?
To live side by side on the earth is to suck one another dry.
   I stand at the kitchen sink at twilight clipping
My fingernails into running water, not in fear of witchcraft
   but of the Board of Health, if they inspected private homes.
In my gut (as in yours, Cleopatra my Empress my Queen) a horde
   of silent germs labor over my recent dinner, processing,
Waging holy war. *God is eternal surfeit*, Heraclitus whispers.
   I have grown too old to dream of whispering, and the grackles
Disdain to weep like their weakling cousin robins,
   and the leaves and the moon have dissolved
Like vinyl records under acid rain in that cardboard box
   I left in a leaky storeroom behind a house I lived in
Thirty years ago, full of rat pellets and moldy fertilizer sacks
   and a tintype of a woman who died a year before
The Civil War: she is playing a parlor guitar
   and maybe humming, she is calcium dust and wax,
A doll with my face, bristling with needles, bearing the secret
   of her life like forgotten music gutting the twilight, vanished now
Into bacteria and potash and a soul particulate as galaxies.

from *Hinchas de Poesía*

Morning Tableau

◊   ◊   ◊

Intermittent drizzle on the orange roofs;
a barge slides russeting water, I awoke
and heard brass music from another century:
carriage tinkles and princes and parasols
the white of souls promenading by the river;
no tankers, no allies, just rows of lindens,
"without the broken crucifixes of swastikas,"
and a cortège of starred-arm people, clasped-hands,
shuffling to the prick of spires, by rote,
a voice terse script silting the sky.

A breeze then shatters the rain's paralysis,
sheets away the corpse barge, lifts mist clear
off the roofs, blanches the sun's fight to copper
the river to my love's rye-colored skin
when she surrenders to summer in a hammock's
sweep on the porch, and I watch over her shifts,
between the inferno and paradise, and hear
my reflection murmuring: my God, my heaven,

my all, and hear the leaves gnashing
where the trees are glinting shades forgetting
their journey to this place of morning.

from *Connotation Press*

Aubade

◇　◇　◇

after R.W.

You could be home boiling a pot
of tea as you sit on your terrace,
reading up on last night's soccer shot
beneath a scarf of cirrus.

You could be diving headlong
into the waves of Cocoa Beach
or teaching Mao Tse-tung
whose theories are easy to reach

or dropping off your dry cleaning,
making the New Americans wealthier,
or mowing your lawn, greening
up, but isn't this healthier?

Just imagine the hours you're
not squandering away,
nor the antlike minutes frittered
with a tentative fiancé.

Your whole body agrees you'd
rather lie here like a snail
in my arm's crook, nude
and oblivious of all emails.

Yes, it's nearly one o'clock,
but we have more reasons

to kiss, to engage in small talk.
For one, these blissful seasons

are short, & tomorrow is never
insured, so bounce downstairs:
pour us glasses of whatever,
a tray of crackers, bosc pears,

then let drop your sarong,
the wind high on your skin,
so we can test all day long
the notion of original sin.

from *The New Yorker*

Visions of Labor

◇   ◇   ◇

I will have writings written all over it
in human words: wrote Blake. A running
form, Pound's Blake: shouting, whirling
his arms, his eyes rolling, whirling like flaming
cartwheels. Put it this way, in this language:
a blow in the small of the back from a rifle butt,
the crack of a blackjack on a skull, face
beaten to a pulp, punched in the nose
with a fist, glasses flying off, "fuckin' Wobblie
wop, hit him again for me," rifle barrel slammed
against the knees, so much blood in the eyes,
rain, and the night, and the shooting pain
all up and down the spine, can't see. Put it
this way: in the sense of smell is an acrid
odor of scorched metal, in the sense of sound,
the roaring of blow torches. Put it in this
language: labor's value is abstract value,
abstracted into space in which a milling machine
cutter cuts through the hand, the end of her thumb
nearly cut off, metal shavings driven in, rapidly
infected. Put it at this point, the point at which
capital is most inhumane, unsentimental,
out of control: the quantity of human labor in
the digital manufacture of a product is progressing
toward the economic value of zero, the maintenance
and monitoring of new cybernetic processes
occupied by fungible, commodified, labor
in a form of indentured servitude. Static model,
dynamic model, alternate contract environments,

enterprise size and labor market functions,
equilibrium characterization, elasticity of response
to productivity shocks: the question in this Third
Industrial Revolution is who owns and controls
the data. That's what we're looking at, labor cheap,
replaceable, self-replicating, marginal, contracted out
into smaller and smaller units. Them? Hordes
of them, of depleted economic, social, value,
who don't count, in any situation, in anyone's eyes,
and won't count, ever, no matter what happens,
the truth that, sooner than later, they will simply be
eliminated. In Hanover Square, a freezing dawn,
from inside bronze doors the watchman sips
bourbon and black coffee in a paper cup, sees
a drunk or drugged hedge fund boy step over
a passed-out body. A logic of exploitation.
A logic of submission. The word alienation. Eyes
being fixed on mediated screens, in semiotic
labor flow: how many generations between
these States' age of slavery and ours? Makers,
we, of perfectly contemplated machines.

from *London Review of Books*

As If

◇   ◇   ◇

As if the corpse behind the crime scene tape
got up and took a bow where it dropped dead;
as if I got a phone call from the grave
and asked its occupant to share my bed.
Nine years ago, we fought and split apart
with our beloved city underwater.
I turned to short-term lovers in the dark;
you moved in with a southern judge's daughter.
I have to pinch myself to prove you're back,
though balder, ten pounds thinner, better dressed—
as if the universe had jumped a track,
no hurricane, no choices second-guessed.
At times my ears pick up the strangest sound,
as if the dead were clapping underground.

from *Cherry Tree*

SUJI KWOCK KIM

Return of the Native

◇　◇　◇

for Kang,
born in Sonchon, North Korea

Better not to have been born
than to survive everyone you loved.

There's no one left of those who lived here once,
no one to accuse you, no one to forgive you—

only beggar boys or black-market wives
haggling over croakers and cuttlefish,

hawking scrap-iron and copper-pipes stripped from factories
in the shadow of the statue of the Great Leader.

Only streets emptied of the villagers you knew,
only the sound of steps of those no longer living,

ghosts grown old, grim shadows of what they had once been:
some in handcuffs, some in hoods taken away at midnight,

some roped and dragged into Soviet Tsir trucks
driven to the labor camps that "don't exist."

Every absence has a name, a face, a fate:
but who, besides you, remembers they were ever alive?

You don't know why you were spared,
why you breathe walk drink eat laugh weep—

never speaking of those who had been killed,
as if they had never existed, as if the act of surviving them

had murdered them.
Forget, forget! But they want to be remembered.

Better people than you were shot:
do you think your life is enough for them?

For the silence
is never silent: it says We hate you

because you survived. No. We hate you
because you escaped.

from *Ploughshares*

Tissue Gallery

◇   ◇   ◇

On the fifth floor
of the medical school,
            sequestered from public view,
    a black slab lab table
lined with old apothecary jars and twist-top jars
        sealed with paraffin wax,
        a shoal of *not-fish* treading bronzy water,
    each homunculus labelled
                in terms of in-utero days and weeks.

In this jarscape, a palm-size one
                        sitting with legs crossed,
        arms raised protectively,
                    clasping the top of his head
    like a child expecting blows in a parental brawl,
and this golem, a perfect mini-person,
            holds fingers curved lightly in front of him,
                    as if playing a piano chord,
        and this *quelque chose* has blackened soles—
                in the womb,
                a *douen* meant to range the barefoot forest,
those faceless stillborn and early-dead children with
    backward feet,
                who lure human playmates to the woods
    and fill their always hungry mouths with little crabs.

All casualties are clipped
                    with yellowed plastic navel clamps
        that look like bones.

Here are twins, one larger than the other,
  one malformed
    with hydrocephalitic-fissured face,
and this one's wrinkly forehead,
    the face of a worried eighty-year-old concentrating
  on his death,   an extra epaulette flap on his shoulder,
        as if he is sprouting wings;
triplets like three piglets,
        one with lots of hair,
one with cauliflower, puckered ear,
    one with a purple-black hand reaching out of the
    water,
      as if in hope to be rescued from drowning.

The thirty-six-weekers are not stored in glassware.
A perfect pair, girl and boy, are on separate cookie baking
  sheets,
    wrapped in sterile pads, their swaddling blankets.
They are not desiccated, withered, mummified,
    quick-frozen, frost-nipped, or sealed in wax.
They look like leatherette dolls in mid-kick stop-motion
  animation,
      as if they'd only now stopped breathing.

Girl was a low birth weight,
    vagina snapped as tightly shut as the seam of a walnut.
Boy is not the color of life, a rich-colored brown boy
        bleached out to plasticine-pale, dun-white.
Still, on his cheek-ear-hair, the almost-feel of life.
      The abdomen is caved in,
    and the testicles are paper-thin, black, crumpled leaves.

Some in the jars were named and tagged on the wrist.
  I was told that I cannot tell you the names.
          It is a secret between the women
          and these medical anomalies.
    One is named for a hurricane.

The *restos muertos* have closed eyes and African features.
    They were not colorfast,

so the chemicals have bleached them to albino.
The women, who came with gravid uterus to Puerto Rico
from the Virgin Islands, seeking to save or end
pregnancies,
do not know that these small ones are still here
curled in their womb poses,
each blanched
in its lit-glass aquarium,
lolling in solvent tinted the color of beer, brandy, honey,
oil, or perfume.

These small floating gods in primer paint, never to be
besprinkled
with blessed water to help them cross over,
never to evaporate, dust-scatter, or waste—they are here
and not here!
What is the shelf life of the unborn?

In the Caribbean, women must travel
from island to island
to get needed health care,
and so these doodads
were not carried home but donated,
no one knows how long ago.

I have been invited here by a doctor who loves the arts,
and whom I like.
I was told beforehand only that I would be viewing
human tissue.
He proposes collaboration, an artistic public exhibition
of these impossible children,
who will never utter "peacock,"
"butterfly,"
"confetti," "crazy quilt," "cashmere," or "soap."

Skullduggery.
Monster Midway. Gaff joints. Shell games. Sideshow
piebald children.
Human oddities and the science of teratology.

At home, I whisper to the midnight page,
Women of the Virgin Islands, *Sistren*,
I saw them, and they are okay.
Your small ones are still on the Earth!

from *The New Yorker*

The Swimmer

◊   ◊   ◊

It was one of those midsummer Sundays . . .
—John Cheever

Photo: sitting by the cabin on Lake Au Train
We rented every summer, reading John Cheever,
Then rowing out in a boat after dinner to fish.
The light would turn golden, then start to fade
As I headed home, past a new log dream house
I could see from our porch, and wished I could own.
I was married then and lived in my imagination,
Writing the poems I was sure would make my name
Eventually, and meanwhile waiting out the afternoons
Within the limits of a world that never changed,

The world of stories. I was almost thirty-eight,
With the compulsion to immortalize myself
That comes with middle age and disappointment.
I knew what I imagined and desired, yet didn't know,
For even though desire can delineate the contours
Of a life, its true substance is beyond desire
And imagination, unrecognizable until it's happened.
In seven years the substance of my future changed:
Instead of summers on the lake, I found myself alone
And free, not wanting what I'd wanted anymore,

And happy. Happiness, unhappy people say,
Comes in degrees, and yet it isn't true. The same
Ambitions and desires, the same attachments
And designs can constitute two different worlds—

A world I'd lived in and a world I never knew
Until I entered it, and made it mine. I wrote a long,
Meandering poem on marriage and its aftermath
That argued (if a poem can argue) that it never ends,
But stays suspended in time, like an afternoon
In August in our small cabin, with the television on

And the lake still visible beyond the door.
It's all still there, in that decade out of mind
I never think about anymore, until some moment
In a movie, or in a story I thought I'd read
And hadn't, or read and can't remember
Brings it back, and then I'm thirty-eight again,
The future still uncertain and there for the taking,
Which is what I did, though I didn't know it—
Which doesn't matter now, for though those wishes
Did come true, it wasn't as I'd dreamed them.

"The Monkey's Paw" is a story about three wishes—
The first one a disaster, the second one an unintended
Horror it takes the last wish to dissolve—that ends
On an empty street. My story is not so dramatic,
Yet the ending feels the same: I have the life
I wanted, people know my name, music fills the rooms
Each evening and each day renews the miracle,
And yet it's not the same. The real world can never
Realize a fantasy lived in the imagination,
That only felt like heaven while it wasn't there.

I thought I'd read "The Swimmer" sitting by the lake
Those thirty-something years ago, but when I looked at it
Last week I couldn't remember reading it at all. It's a story
Devastating on its face—an allegory of the dissolution
Of its hero, who on a beautiful suburban afternoon
Sets out for home by way of swimming pools and alcohol.
His quest begins in confidence and gladness, but as its course
Unfolds its tenor starts to change, as the watercolor
Light begins to fade, the air turns colder and he ages visibly,
Until it ends in autumn, darkness and an empty house.

The moral of the allegory is implicit, but it seems to me
More moving read another way—as a reimagining
Of a life from the perspective of disillusionment and age.
It still starts on a summer afternoon, but a remembered one.
Instead of youth and confidence and hope dissolving,
They're already gone, and instead of a deteriorating world,
It's an indifferent one. I feel at home in this amended parable:
It fits the way a story ought to fit, and it even feels true.
Sitting in my house in the country, there isn't much to do
But stare at the trees through the patio doors open to the deck.

It's not the dream house I remember, but at least it's mine,
And at least I'm happy, though I've lately come to recognize
That happiness is not what it's cracked up to be. As for poetry,
Poetry turned out fine, though nobody actually cares about it
In the old sense anymore. That's the trouble with stories—
They need to come to a conclusion and to have a point,
Whereas the point of growing old is that it doesn't have one:
Someone sets out on an afternoon, following his predetermined
Course as all around him summer darkens and the leaves turn sere,
And finally arrives at home, and finds there's nothing there.

from *The Paris Review*

The Fool

◊　◊　◊

C'mon, Your Majesty, her brother?
I know the scent of belladonna
can poison a mind, even a king's,
but would you dare to behead
your own nightmares? Now,
I hope you are more than pewter
& pallor. Where is the early heart
I gladly remember from the days
I hailed as your father's cutthroat?
I know hearsay can undo a kingdom.
I never cursed your tower guards
& I dare translate their foofaraw.
I double swear on the good book
though I could be our Shagspere
or William Kemp paying his tab
with a proud penny & a plug nickel.
Your Highness, only a horsewhip
could heal my unnatural tongue,
that is, if you consent to be the first
flogged up & down the castle steps.
After the guillotine & a coronation,
you would think a king too weak
to properly father a son & heir,
in the unholy days of the masque.
My queen, today, my lovely queen
singing wildly behind an iron door,
her head ready for your oak block,

holds now her lame bird in a box
of twigs, a toy against eternity.

from *Tin House*

We drive home from the lake, sand in our shoes,

◊ ◊ ◊

the dart of fish faint at our ankles, each
shuttered BBQ shack a kudzu flash

in my side mirror. Pleasure has become
the itch of a mosquito bite between

my shoulders, and your rough thumb on my thigh
a tickle gentle as turtles bobbing

in Sea-Doo oil slick and cellophane scraps.
How many years did I suffer the loves

that gave too much freedom and not enough
tenderness? Let me be like the man we

saw outside of Notasulga, hands cuffed
behind his back, cigarette in his mouth,

and you be the sheriff, leaning in close,
cupping the sweet flame to my waiting face.

from *Gulf Coast*

Solitaire

◊ ◊ ◊

That summer there was no girl left in me.
It gradually became clear.
It suddenly became.

In the pool, I was more heavy than light. Pockmarked and
flabby in a floppy hat.
What will my body be

when parked all night in the earth?
Midsummer. Breathe in. Breathe out.
I am not on the oxygen tank.

Twice a week we have sex.
The lithe girls poolside I see them
at their weddings I see them with babies their hips

thickening I see them middle-aged.
I can't see past the point where I am.
Like you, I'm just passing through.

I want to hold on awhile.
Don't want to naught
or forsake, don't want

to be laid gently or racked raw.
If I retinol. If I marathon.
If I Vitamin C. If I crimson

my lips and streakish my hair.
If I wax. Exfoliate. Copulate
beside the fish-slicked sea.

Fill me I'm cold. Fill me I'm halfway gone.
Would you crush me in the stairwell?
Could we just lie down?

If the brakes don't work.
If the pesticides won't wash off.
If the seventh floor pushes a brick

out the window and it lands on my head.
If a tremor, menopause. Cancer. ALS.
These are the ABCs of my fear.

The doctor says
I don't have a pill for that, dear.
Well, what would be a cure-all, ladies,

gin-and-tonics on a summer night?
See you in the immortalities! O blurred.
O tumble-rush of days we cannot catch.

from *The New Yorker*

Folding a Five-Cornered Star So the Corners Meet

◇ ◇ ◇

This sadness I feel tonight is not my sadness.

Maybe it's my father's.
For having never been prized by his father.
For having never profited by his son.

This loneliness is Nobody's. Nobody's lonely
because Nobody was never born
and will never die.

This gloom is Someone Else's.
Someone Else is gloomy
because he's always someone else.
For so many years, I answered to a name,
and I can't say who answered.

Mister Know Nothing? Brother Inconsolable?
Sister Every Secret Thing? Anybody? Somebody?

Somebody thinks:
With death for a bedfellow,
how could thinking be anything but restless?
Somebody thinks: *God, I turn my hand face down*
and You are You and I am me.

I turn my hand face up
and You are the I
and I am your Thee.

What happens when you turn your hand?

Lord, remember me.
I was born in the City of Victory,
on a street called Jalan Industri, where
each morning, the man selling rice cakes went by
pushing his cart, its little steamer whistling,
while at his waist, at the end of a red string,
a little brass bell
shivered into a fine, steady seizure.

This sleeplessness is not my sleeplessness.
It must be the stars' insomnia.
And I am their earthbound descendant.

Someone, Anyone, No one, me, and Someone Else.
Five in a bed, and none of us can sleep.
Five in one body, begotten, not made.
And the sorrow we bear together is none of ours.
Maybe it's Yours, God.
For living so near to your creatures.
For suffering so many incarnations unknown to Yourself.
For remaining strange to lovers and friends,
and then outliving them and all of their names for You.
For living sometimes for years without a name.
And all of Your spring times disheveled.
And all of Your winters one winter.

from *Image*

More Than You Gave

◊   ◊   ◊

We have the town we call home wakening for dawn
which isn't yet here but is promised, we have

our tired neighbors rising in ones and twos, we have
the sky slowly separating itself from the houses

to become the sky while the stars blink a last time
and vanish to make way for us to enter the great stage

of an ordinary Tuesday in ordinary time. We have
our curses, our gripes, our lies all on the stale breath

of 6:37 A.M. in the city no one dreams, the Tuesday city
in which we shall live for this day or not at all.

"Where are the angels?" I ask. This is a visionary moment
in the history of time, incomplete without angels,

without at least Argente of the tarnished wings,
or the mangled half-assed Incondante who speaks

only in riddles, or one-winged Sylvania who glows
in the dark. All off in eternity doing their sacred numbers.

Instead at 6:43 A.M. we have Vartan Baghosian with a face
seamed like a softball and Minky Schantz who pitched

three games for the Toledo Mud Hens in '39 and lost
them all, we have the Volpe sisters who married

the attic on Brush Street and won't come down,
we have me, fresh as last week, bitching about my back,

my bad ankle, we have psoriasis, heartburn, the four-day
hangover, prostatitis, Jewish mothers, Catholic guilt,

we have the teenage Woodward Ave. whores going
to bed alone at last, hugging no one for that long moment

before the young Madonnas rise from separate beds
to open their shutters on whatever the day presents,

to pledge their virtue and their twitching, incomparable bodies
to Jesus Christ of the Latter Day Tupperware. All this

in rooms where even in the gray dishwater dawn
the chrome grill on an Admiral black-and-white TV

gleams like the chalice of Abraham. And from his corner
the genius of this time and place, Uncle Nate, chomping

his first White Owl of the day, calls out for a doughnut
and sweetened milky coffee to dunk it in and laces up

his high-tops and swears by the vision of his blind right eye
he will have strange young pussy before the sun sets

on his miserable balding dome. Today we shall paint,
for Nate is a true artist trained in the eight-hour day

to master the necessary and not the strung-out martyrs
of El Greco or the brooding landscapes of an awful century.

No, today we paint the walls, the lintels, the ceilings,
the dadoes, and the doodads of Mrs. Victoria Settle

formerly of Lake Park, Illinois, now come to grace
our city with the myth of her late husband, her terriers,

her fake accent, her Victorian brooches, her perfect posture,
and especially her money. Ask the gray windows

that look out on the remnants of winter a grand question:
"Have I come all the way through the fires of hell,

the torture of the dark night of the etc., so that I might inhale
the leaden fumes of Giddens Golden Gate as the dogsbody

of Nathaniel Hawthorne Glenner, the autodidact of Twelfth Street?"
It could be worse. It could be life without mortadella sandwiches,

twenty-five-cent pineapple pies, and quarts of Pilsner
at noon out on a manicured lawn in Grosse Pointe

under a sun that never before caressed an Armenian or a Jew.
We could be flogging Fuller brushes down the deadbeat streets

of Paradise Valley or delivering trunks to the dormitories
of the Episcopal ladies where no one tips or offers

a pastry and a schnapps for the longed-for trip
back to Sicily or Salonika; it could be the forge room

at Ford Rouge where the young get old fast or die trying.
So savor the hours as Nate recounts the day he hitchhiked

to Toledo only to arrive too late to see the young Dempsey
flatten Willard and claim the lily-white championship

of the world. "Story of my life," says Nate, "the last to arrive,
the first to leave." Not even Aesop could outdo our Nate,

our fabulist, whose name even is pure invention,
a confabulation of his prison reading and his twelve-year

formal education in the hobo camps of his long boyhood.
Wanderlust, he tells us, hit him at age fifteen and not

a moment too soon for Mr. Wilson was taking boys
off to die in Europe and that was just about the time

women discovered Nate or Nate discovered women,
and they were something he wouldn't care to go without.

Call it a long day if you want and a hard one, too,
but remember we got more than we gave: we got myth,

we got music, we got underpaid work, a cheap lunch
with more to follow. On the long walk to the bus stop

and the ride home we hear the birds gathering
in the elms and maples thickening with summer finery,

and no one cares if we sing to the orange sun
that also seeks its rest, no one cares that our voices

are harsh from cigarettes and our ears worthless,
our timing off, and we've got the wrong words

in the wrong places. Let's just give it what we have
and when that's done give it a second time, one

for us and one for Nate, and even a third wouldn't hurt.

from *The New Yorker*

If He Came & Diminished Me & Mapped My Way

◊   ◊   ◊

Who was there in the uncountable stars, in the distance,
And in the cold glittering?
Who leaned with the wind against the trees all day,

And who slept in the swing's empty stillness under them?

Who was present in the pattern of the snake fading
Into the pattern of the leaves again?

And who presided over the empty clarity of water falling,
Water spreading into a thin, white veil
Glimpsed just once in a moment clear & empty as a heaven—

Once heaven has been swept clean of any meaning?

Whose childhood is no more than a blackened rafter,
Something left after fire has swept through it?

*

It is years later when I come back to that place where I'd hiked once,
And somehow lost the trail, & then,
For a while, walked in the Company of Hallucination & Terror,

And noted afterward, like something closing within me,

That slight disappointment when I found

The trail again, when the rocks & trees took
Their places beside it, & I went on, up
To the summit of bare rock & the smoke rising

Lazily out of the small hut there, soup & coffee,
A table of brochures & maps of hiking trails

I browsed through idly, recalling being lost,
Recalling the way each rock looked, how
Expressionless it was, how each

Was the same as another, without a face, until
I understood I was completely lost, & then
How someone so thin I could have passed my hand through him

Walked beside me there, & though I did not dare look
To see who it was, I glanced sideways once to see

How his ribs depicted famine, & how his steps beside me

Were effortless, were like air gliding through air
Again & again without haste or hesitation

As the trail appeared again under my feet & rose
Upward in a long series of switchbacks

Through a forest I no longer believed in.

What I felt was diminishment, embarrassment, &

He must be starving by now, his face multiplying
To become the haunted faces of others in the streets,

Where to walk at night is to be flayed alive beneath

The freezing rain, where the trees glisten with ice,
And the lights are left on all night in the big stores,

If the pleasure of his company does not last,
If the terror of his company does not last,
If forgetting or remembering him are the same, now,

As I slow the car, pull over to the curb,
And wait until I see my dealer emerge
Cautiously as always from the fenced walkway beside

An abandoned house in a street of abandoned,
Or nearly vacant & for sale, houses,

And if, by getting high, one can live
Effortlessly anywhere for a little while, if

Me & my dealer, a Jamaican named John Donne,

Gaze out at the rain & listen to the hushed clatter
Of an empty metal shopping cart someone pushes through the rain,

If we gaze out at the living, & at the dead, & they are the same,
If the sound of a bus going past & the sound of the wind

Are the same, are what is left to listen to in the world,

Though the world sleeps, & the trees above us sleep, their limbs
Mending themselves in the cold wind,

Then both of Us would avert our Faces from His Face.

from *The Southern Review*

ROBIN COSTE LEWIS

On the Road
to Sri Bhuvaneshwari

◊　◊　◊

Not much larger than a Volkswagen. Smiling
　　on the dashboard: Gurumukh. Marigolds
　　　　so mild we can chew. What we call *mountain*
　　　　　　they say *foothill*. A whole vibrant green

valley of terraced balconies, rectangular
　　rice farms carved into every façade
　　　　for seven centuries. Now and then
　　　　　　a clay road washed out by rain. We wait.

Barefoot men in madras dhotis, bodies
　　large only as necessity, hoist twice that in boulders
　　　　back up the mountain, back to that place
　　　　　　where the road had been.

Monsoon. Uttar Pradesh. Twenty-eight days of rain.
　　At dinner, someone says, During
　　　　the nineteenth century, all this water
　　　　　　caused the British to go

mad. They constantly committed suicide.
　　Later, someone else
　　　　points out their Victorian cemetery.
　　　　　　I smile—a little.

That morning, seven langurs the size of six-
        year-olds, gray and brown, white and beige, tall tails
            curling, jumped up and down, shucked
                and jived on top of my cold tin roof.

Somehow, I am still alive.
        I know it is wrong
            to think of a decade as lost.
                The more I recover, the more I go

blind. Squat
        naked beside a steaming bucket.
            Hold a small cloth.
                In Trinidad, one says *clot*.

The *h* is quiet.
        A wafer of breath—just
            like here. There's no telling
                what languishes inside the body.

Not mist, but a whole cloud
        passes into one window,
            then two hours later,
                out the other.

The American college students try out
        their kindergarten Hindi: *ha-pee-tal*,
            ha-pee-tal. Lips finger the sign's script,
                then the United States break

open their mouths
        into sad smiles when they realize
            it's not Hindi, but English
                written in Devanagari: *hospital*.

For the whole day we drive
        along miles of wet, slithering clay
            to find a temple at the top of a *mountain*
                where Shiva is said to have once dropped

a piece of Parvati.
      Every mountaintop made holy
          by the falling charred body part
             of the Goddess. An elbow fell

here; here
      fell Her toe; an ankle—black
          and burnt—Her knee. The road is wet and dark
             red, and keeps spinning.

I sit behind the driver, admiring
      his cinnamon fingers, his coiffed white beard,
          his pale pink turban wrapped so handsomely.
             Why did it take all that?

I mean, why did She have to jump
      into the celestial fire
          to prove Her purity?
             Shiva's cool—poisonous, blue,

a shimmering galaxy—
      but when it came to His Old Lady,
          man, He fucked up!
             Why couldn't He just believe Her?

I joke with the driver. We laugh.
      Gurumukh smiles back. But then I think, perhaps
          embodiment is so bewildering, even God grows
             wracked with doubt.

For a certain amount
      of rupees, the temple's hired a man
          to announce to tourists . . . *During the medieval period*
             virgins were sacrificed here.

His capitalist glance mirrors our Orientalist tans.
      You're lying, I say. *Save it*
          for somebody pale. He smiles, passes
             me a beedi. I'm bleeding, but lie

so I can go inside
      and see that burnt, charred
            piece of the Goddess that fell off
               right here.

We climb up another one hundred
      and eight stairs. At the top, I try
            not to listen to anyone.
               An entire Himalayan valley. Chiseled.

Every mountain—peak to base—
      a living terraced verdant staircase
            for the Goddess to walk down:
            Sri Bhuvaneshwari.

ii.

At night, our caravan winds back
      over gravel and clay. Ten headlamps
            grope the mountain walls
               of the green-black valley. The road

is only as wide as one small car. Hours of dog
      elbows, switchbacks, half roads.
            Slowly after a turn, the driver takes his foot
               off the gas, downshifts, coasts.

Black. Warm. Breath. Snorting.
      Our car rubs against one biting grass off the face
            of a cliff. Then another, taller
               than our car. Then hundreds

block the road. Thick cylindrical horns scrape
      the driver's window; eyes so white, black
            pupils gleam, peering into our cab, grunting
               and drooling onto the window.

Now the whole car, surrounded. Warm black bodies
        covered in fur. Near their dusty hooves, children
                sit on the ground, nested in laps, quiet and smiling.
                Everyone embroidered with color:

silvers, metallic ochres, kohls, golds, reds, bold
        blacks, all of it—and a green so green
                I realize it's a hue
                I have never seen.

A whole nomadic clan, traveling
        with hundreds of water buffalo. At least
                sixty human beings. There are so many
                        buffalo, our cars cannot move. And they can't move

the herd because a few feet ahead
        a She-Buffalo is giving birth.
                We get out.
                And wait.

Out of habit, the students pull out their American sympathy,
        but then the driver says all the women sitting there
                on the ground, dusty, with children in their laps, dangling
                        their ankles over the mountain, adorned—all—

wear enough gold, own enough
        buffalo to buy your whole house—cash.
                The night holds. Life is giving birth
                        in the middle of a warm dark road.

Everyone in our party waits, smiling and gesturing
        with the whole clan, surrounded by snoring
                black bodies taller than our chins. We squat
                        beside their lanterns, stand inside our headlight.

The driver, who grew up in this valley,
        speaks two dialects, four national languages, plus English,
                cannot understand a single word anyone says.
                Solid gold bangles, thick as bagels;

diamonds so large and rough they look
      like large cubes of clear glass. The women stare through
          their bright syllables. Then one lifts her hand, points
              at one of us—says something—and they all laugh.

iii.

The calf is born dead. A folded and wet black nothing.
      It falls out of its mother—still—onto the ground.
          We watch it in the headlamps. Empty fur sack.
              A broken umbrella made of blood and bone.

The mother tries to run. Several men hold her, throw
      broad coils of rope around her hooves. Two men, barefoot
          in dhotis, grab her on each side by her horns. And wait.
              They wait through her heaving. They sing

to her, they coo. Men who are midwives. Through
      four translations, they say it is her first time.
          She must turn around and see
              what has happened to her, or she will go mad.

We wait with the whole tribe, wait with the whole night, wait
      for her to stop bucking. Her hip bones
          are as tall as my eyes. Her neck is a massive drum.
              They do not force her, but they will not let her run.

She is pinned to the mountain, her black flat tail points down
      toward her dead newborn. There are four hands
          on her wide horns; four more hold the ropes
              that surround her haunches.

Finally, after half an hour
      of bucking and grunting, she drops her eyes
          and gives. She lowers her face into it—into the black
              slick dead thing folded on the ground—

and sniffs. Nudges the body. Snorts.
       Then they let her go. She runs off, back
           into the snoring herd.
              Disappears.

iv.

One day, ten years later—one fine, odd day—suddenly
       I will remember all of this. That night, that dark
           narrow road will come back. Like a small sleepy child, it will sit
              gently down inside my lap, and look up into me.

Kohl and camphor around all the babies' eyes
       to keep evil away; that exquisite smell of men
           and sweat and dust; the unanticipated calm
             of standing within

an enormous herd of sleeping water buffalo, listening.
       To spend your entire life—out of doors—walking the world
           with your whole family and neighborhood. To stay
              together, to leave together. *What a blessing*, I think,

and then, *What a curse!*
       My newborn is asleep in a red wagon
           that says *Radio Flyer*. I have packed
             a large suitcase and one box.

The World wants to know
       what I am made of. I am trying
           to find a way
             to answer Her.

I place our things by the door. And wait.
       Standing. Eyes closed. Looking. I want to
           remember the carved angels flying over the tall bay
             windows; the front door's twelve perfect squares

of beveled glass; the cloud-high ceilings;
      the baby's stuffed monkey; the tribal rugs; and the photograph
          of our tent in the desert that one soundless morning, on the floor
            of a canyon in Jordan. All in boxes now.

The lights are on. The house
      is empty. Night comes.
          I smell the giant magnolia blossoms
            opening.

Once, I thought I was a person with a body,
      the body of something peering
          out, enchanted
            and tossed.

The baby wakes. He is almost four
      weeks old. I give him a piece
          of my body. He fingers my necklace
            strung with green glass beads.

I tie him onto my back and think about the brazen
      dahlias, nursed from seeds, staging a magenta riot now,
          next to the rusty Victorian daybed, where he was conceived,
            beneath the happy

banana tree out on the back balcony.
      My father's gold earrings are welded into my ears.
      My mother's diamonds are folded
          into a handkerchief inside my pocket.

And then, as if
      it is the most natural thing to do, I walk
          toward the stairwell, and give
            the World my answer.

All the way down the staircase, my hand palms
      the mahogany rail, and I think, Once
          this beam of wood stood high
            inside a great dark forest.

v.

Thick coat. Black fur. Two russet horns
    twisted to stone. One night
        I was stuck on a narrow road,
            panting.

I was pregnant.
    I was dead.
        I was a fetus.
            I was just born

(Most days
    I don't know what I am).
    I am a photograph
        of a saint, smiling.

For years, my whole body ran
    away from me. When I flew—charred—
        through the air, my ankles and toes fell off
            onto the peaks of impassable mountains.

I have to go back
    to that wet black thing
        dead in the road. I have to turn around.
        I must put my face in it.

It is my first time.
    I would not have it any other way.
    I am a valley of repeating
        verdant balconies.

from *Los Angeles Review of Books*

THOMAS LUX

Ode While Awaiting Execution

◊　◊　◊

Into the mute and blue-
green marble mailbox my dust deserves to go,
though not for that which I'm going.
I deserve to go, and not alone,
because I did not sing loud enough
about this life, this world.
Singing poorly is acceptable. Not loud enough is not.
There were too many things I saw
of which I did not sing, things raw
and eyeball-vibrating ravishing, or worse, things I forgot,
until a pin-stick shock, a creak
in a house of wood waking to heat,
or a bent nail remembered for me.
How did Spinoza define happiness?
Patient acceptance of the inevitable?
I find my self *im*-
patient. I'm *often* impatient. Not for the inevitable,
which can wait patiently for me.
So far, the Governor's not called the Warden,
whose palm has an itch.
He prefers an electrical switch.
My lawyers, having, in law, no degrees,
are not allowed in to counsel me.
Appeals are exhausted, or at least very tired.
So, I scratch this out on my last yellow legal pad's last
page: I deserve to go,
but not for that which

I'll lie on a table
and get the needle.

from *Ploughshares*

PAUL MARIANI

Psalm for the Lost

◊   ◊   ◊

Down the dark way, the dark way down.
Everything dark now, as he has come to see:
that the way was always dark, the journey dark,
the mind dark, the answers like the questions
dark, each day dark, the glaucous pearl white eyes,
even when the sun spread across the greengold grass
glistening the bright skin of the copper beeches.

★

Dark, dark, and dark. Because it is the nature
of the restless mind which knows too well
that nothing is ever really known, no matter
how much one tells oneself it is. The books,
the words: all so much straw, even when
they seemed to blaze with meaning. One
more piece, he used to think, one more shard

to complete the puzzle, even as it all
slipped down the drain, the vortex
of the drain, dark, dark and dark. And it was night,
John says, the light departed, the face distorted
in the brazier's glow. I know him not. Yes,
I knew him once, and the sunlight sang. But that
was then, you have to understand. That was then,

★

before the answers like the very questions ceased
to call out to each other. Yes, that was then, when I built
my castle by the sea in the bright mid-morning sun,
and thought that what I'd made was good, before
the indifferent tide came rolling in again, dissolving
everything. Dark, dark, oh dark. And nothing for it
but to let the wind rebuild it, bit by bit, and lift it as it will.

from *Image*

DEBRA MARQUART

Lament

◇   ◇   ◇

north dakota   i'm worried about you
the companies you keep   all these new friends   north dakota
     beyond the boom, beyond the precious resources
          do you really think they care what becomes of you

north dakota   you used to be the shy one
enchanted secret land loved by only a few   north dakota

when i traveled away and told people i belonged to you   north dakota
     your name rolled awkwardly from their tongues
          a mouth full of rocks, the name of a foreign country

north dakota   you were the blushing wallflower
the natural beauty, nearly invisible, always on the periphery
north dakota   *the least visited state in the union*

now everyone knows your name   north dakota
the blogs and all the papers are talking about   you even *60 minutes*
i'm collecting your clippings   north dakota
the pictures of you from space
     the flares of natural gas in your northern corner
          like an exploding supernova
               a massive city where no city exists
                    a giant red blight upon the land

and those puncture wounds   north dakota   take care of yourself
the injection sites   I've see them on the maps
thousands of active wells   one every two miles

108

all your indicators are up   north dakota
        four hundred billion barrels, some estimates say

more oil than we have water to extract
        more oil than we have atmosphere to burn

north dakota   you could run the table right now   you could write your ticket
        so, how can i tell you this?   north dakota, your politicians

            are co-opted (or cowards or bought-out or honest and thwarted)
                    they're lowering the tax rate for oil companies
                    they're greasing the wheels that need no greasing
                    they're practically giving the water away

north dakota   dear sleeping beauty   please, wake up
they have opened you up and said, *come in   take everything*

            what will become of your sacred places,
            what will become of the prairie dog,
            the wolf, the wild horses, the eagle,
            the meadowlark, the fox, the elk,
            the pronghorn antelope, the rare mountain lion,
            the roads, the air, the topsoil,
            your people, your people,
            what will become of the water?

north dakota   who will ever be able to live with you
once this is all over   i'm speaking to you now
as one wildcat girl   to another   be careful   north dakota

                        from *New Letters*

High School in Schuzou

◇   ◇   ◇

They play Ping-Pong. They are all boys. They play
Ping-Pong ceaselessly in the vast gymnasium, will
not stop to glance at us visitors from the West, will
not untie their eyes from the tiny ball. The principal

of the school, salamandered-slick hair, is displeased
the visiting professors are female, leads us out from
the gymnasium with silent loathing to a mentholated
room inside which a hazed Plexiglas cage contains

a stiff leopard, so frankly dead its fur looks as if it'll
fall off from the stroke of our glance. I have to pee.
In the girls' room, I squat where thousands of girls
have squatted, the rich minerals wafting up from

the toilet's well, imagine how all of our urine moves
through the mysterious pipes below, leaves the high
school, depositing itself into the river that days later
I'll move along with the throng of idiots I've joined

to crawl this country as fleas do a dog. We visit one
scholar's garden after another: here's the Garden of
the Master of Nets. The rocks are *bones of the earth.*
The furniture is referred to *internal organs.* Gardens

are *traditionally entered through a narrow passage.*
Scholars were not girls. Girls are not scholars, though
girls are gardens entered through a narrow passage.
The girls at the textile factory we tour do not look up.

The guide snorts. We have no conception how lucky
they are to have attained these jobs! It's only natural
they wear masks to protect their lungs. In high school,
I was the Master of Endless Failures, thrashed nightly

in bed, on the verge of coughing my lungs out, in that
Garden of Spitting Up. And didn't every girl have her
garden? The Garden of Jutting Neck-Bones. Gardens
Pocked with Black Eyes. The Garden of Letting Him

in Despite Many Protests. A dead leopard relentlessly
sheds its fur above an auditorium of children hurtling
toward adulthood. In that gymnasium, there were no
girls playing Ping-Pong. They are all boys, ceaselessly.

from *New England Review*

Everything Will Be Taken Away

◇ ◇ ◇

after Adrian Piper

You can't stop mourning
everything all the time.

The '90s, the black Maxima with a tail,
CD wrappers, proximity to the earth.

Glamour and sweating in your sheets.
Speaking tongues. JLo even. Men even.

You are a woman now
but you have always had skin.

Here are some ways in which
you are not free: the interiors

are all wrong, you are a drought
sprawling. When you see god

you don't like what you see.
It is never enough to be born

again and again.

You like it at church when
strangers hold your hand.

You have a mouth men bless.
You look good enough to bury.

from *Paperbag*

HAI-DANG PHAN

My Father's "Norton Introduction to Literature," Third Edition (1981)

◊   ◊   ◊

Certain words give him trouble: *cannibals, puzzles, sob,*
bosom, martyr, deteriorate, shake, astonishes, vexed, ode . . .
These he looks up and studiously annotates in Vietnamese.
Ravish means *cướp đoạt; shits* is Like when you have to *đi ia;*
mourners are those whom we say are full of *buồn rầu.*
For "even the like precurse of feared events" think *báo trước.*

Its thin translucent pages are webbed with his marginalia,
graphite ghosts of a living hand, and the notes often sound
just like him: "All depend on how look at thing," he pencils
after "I first surmised the Horses' Heads / Were toward Eternity—"
His slanted handwriting is generally small, but firm and clear.
His pencil is a No. 2, his preferred Hi-Liter, arctic blue.

I can see my father trying out the tools of literary analysis.
He identifies the "turning point" of "The Short and Happy Life
of Francis Macomber"; underlines the simile in "Both the old man
and the child stared ahead <u>as if</u> they were awaiting an apparition."
My father, as he reads, continues to notice relevant passages
and to register significant reactions, but increasingly sorts out

his ideas in English, shaking off those Vietnamese glosses.
1981 was the same year we *vượt biển* and came to America,
where my father took Intro Lit ("for fun"), Comp Sci ("for job").
"Stopping by Woods on a Snowy Evening," he murmurs
something about the "dark side of life how awful it can be"
as I begin to track silence and signal to a cold source.

Reading Ransom's "Bells for John Whiteside's Daughter,"
a poem about a "young girl's death," as my father notes,
how could he not have been "<u>vexed</u> at her brown study /
Lying so primly propped," since he never properly observed
(I realize this just now) his own daughter's wake.
Lấy làm ngạc nhiên về is what it means to be astonished.

Her name was Đông Xưa, Ancient Winter, but at home she's Bebe.
"There was such speed in her <u>little body,</u> / And such lightness
in her footfall, / It is no wonder her brown study / Astonishes
us all." In the photo of her that hangs in my parents' house
she is always fourteen months old and staring into the future.
In "reeducation camp" he had to believe she was alive

because my mother on visits "took arms against her shadow."
Did the memory of those days sweep over him like a leaf storm
from the pages of a forgotten autumn? Lost in the margins,
I'm reading the way I discourage my students from reading.
But this is "how we deal with death," his black pen replies.
Assume there is a reason for everything, instructs a green asterisk.

Then between pp. 896–97, opened to Stevens's "Sunday Morning,"
I pick out a newspaper clipping, small as a stamp, an old listing
from the 404-Employment Opps State of Minnesota, and read:
For current job opportunities dial (612) 297-3180. Answered 24 hrs.
When I dial, the automated female voice on the other end
informs me I have reached a nonworking number.

from *Poetry*

The First Last Light
in the Sky

◊   ◊   ◊

That on the silent horizon, something
Not a sunrise rose, half itself and half
The horizon, dragging its bulk, its lights
And salts, from under shifting sheets of sea,
Leveling the sky into shallow moats
Of sounds, flecks of birds, beginning again
To believe all brief and sideways dreaming
To be, as previous was the complaint,
Lint on time's black coat, blanketing the west,
Becoming the unfathomable death mask
Freckled with stars, rendering itself
As its other, as though to mirror la,
But not mirroring it, and therefore now
Mirroring it, all sumptuous unscripted
La, la mirroring la like the pricked prong
Of a tuning fork that, for all its song,
Between sensation and sensation is
Still nothing but air, a titan's dying
Air, a titan's dying air now again
A titan's surging flame, an ancient flinch
In an ancient sun mirrored and made
Into la, the void in the voice, the voice
In the void, lala: aiai, song and pain,
Song and pain, song and pain, and there it is.

from *The Common*

Variation on a Line from Elizabeth Bishop's "Five Flights Up"

◊   ◊   ◊

Sometimes it's the shoes, the tying and untying,
the bending of the heart to put them on,
take them off, the rush of blood
between the head and feet, my face,
sometimes, if I could see it, astonished.
Other times the stairs, three, four stages
at the most, "flights" we call them,
in honor of the wings we'll never have,
the fifth floor the one that kills the breath,
where the bird in the building flies to first.
Love, too, a leveler, a dying all its own,
the parts left behind not to be replaced,
a loss ongoing, and every day increased,
like rising in the night, at anytime a.m.,
to watch the snow or the dead leaf fall,
the rings around the streetlight in the rain,
and then the rain, the red fist in the heart
opening and closing almost without me.
"—Yesterday brought to today so lightly!"
The morning, more and more, like evening.
When I bend to tie my shoes and the blood
fills the cup, it's as if I see into the hidden earth,
see the sunburned path on which I pass
in shoes that look like sandals

and arrive at a house where my feet
are washed and wiped with my mother's hair
and anointed with the autumn oils of wildflowers.

from *Poetry*

JAMES RICHARDSON

Late Aubade

◊　◊　◊

after Hardy

So what do you think, Life, it seemed pretty good to me,
though quiet, I guess, and unspectacular.
It's been so long, I don't know any more how these things go.
I don't know what it means that we've had this time together.

I get that the coffee, the sunlight on glassware, the Sunday paper
and our studious lightness, not hearing the phone, are iconic
of living regretless in the Now. A Cool that's beyond me:
I'm having some trouble acting suitably poised and ironic.

It's sensible to be calm, not to make too much of a little thing
and just see what happens, as I think you are saying
with your amused look, sipping and letting me monologue,
and young as you are, Life, you would know: you have done it all.

If I get up a little reluctantly, tapping my wallet, keys, tickets,
I'm giving you time to say *Stay, it's a dream*
that you're old—no one notices—years never happened—
but I see you have already given me all that you can.

Those clear eyes are ancient; you've done this with billions of others,
but you are my first life, Life; I feel helplessly young.
I'm a kid checking mail, a kid on his cell with his questions:
are we in love, Life, are we exclusive, are we forever?

from *The Yale Review*

At the Tribunals

◇   ◇   ◇

Once, in a brawl on Orchard I clocked a kid
with a ridgehand so hard I could feel

his top teeth give. His knees buckled
and my homeboy let loose a one-two

to finish the job. I turned around
to block a sucker punch that didn't come.

We ducked under the cops' bright red
hatchets that swung around the corner.

I never saw the first kid drop. He must
have been still falling when I dipped

from the scene and trotted toward
Delancey. He was falling when I stopped

to check my leather for scuff marks.
He was falling when I slipped inside

a dive to hide from a girl who got ghost
for books. He was falling when I kissed

the Santo Niño's white feet and Melanie's
left collarbone and the forehead

of one punk whose nose I busted
for nothing but squaring off with me,

his head snapped back to show his neck's
smooth pelt. Look away long enough

and a boy can fall for weeks—decades—
even as you get down on one knee

to pray the rotting kidneys in your mom's
gut don't turn too quick to stone.

I didn't stick around to watch
my own work. I didn't wait for

a single body to hit the pavement.
In those days, it was always spring

and I was mostly made of knives.
I rolled twenty-two deep, every

one of us lulled by a blade
though few of us knew the steel note

that chimed a full measure if you slid
the edge along a round to make it

keen. I'll tell those stiffs in frocks
to go ahead and count me among

the ones who made nothing good
with his bare hands. I'll confess,

I loved the wreckage: no matter
the country, no matter the machine.

from *New England Review*

D A V I D   S T .   J O H N

Vineyard

◇   ◇   ◇

You see a man walking the lanes & aisles
   of his vineyard & now

The spring tendrils stretch beyond his reach
   & you see too there's a black dog

Beside him a blissful Lab who slices across
   a horizon still white with dawn

You see this landscape is the landscape of
   my valley the one I remember

Out of the plunder that is the swollen glow
   of reflection & so to you I'll say

That a man is walking & I'll tell you now he's
   an older man & do you see his son

Behind him only nineteen or twenty no more his
   wool sweater wrapped

Around him the color of the dust at his fee'
   a rich gold without equal

& now the sun begins to rub itself across
   the sky & this is the dog's life

Yet also the man's as well & he knows soon
   this boy will be leaving the valley

With a girl even younger than his son
in a silver Pontiac LeMans

North along Highway 99 north all the way
until they cross into Canada

Where anyone who wants to send his son
to die won't be able to find him

& so there among the aisles & lanes & heavy
grapes the father stops & the dog

Stops to turn & face the boy who drags a hand
slowly along the Lab's silky head

& quietly wraps his skinny arms around his father
& in the vineyard dust that's all

from *The Southern Review*

But I'm the Only One

◊   ◊   ◊

who'll walk across the fire for you,
growled Melissa. That song
blared out from all four of
our bedrooms' tape decks,
often simultaneously, as if
that song was the only one
we all loved, the only one we
could agree on that summer
in the dyke loft, just when it
all started to change. Catherine
was moving out, to SoHo to
live with Melanie. So Shigi's
girlfriend DM took her room.
But not for long; they broke up
and Michelle moved in, shortly
after Cynthia came. *Tonight you
told me that you ache for something
new.* This was way before we'd
even dreamed we'd have to rent
out Shigi's office to Erin as a fifth
bedroom. Without Catherine we
couldn't afford the loft, but we
didn't know that yet. At the time
we thought everyone was poor
like us—we weren't the only ones.
We all smoked constantly, anyone
could afford to smoke back then.
Catherine bummed my last butt
but I know I saw her new carton

in the freezer. She didn't want
to open it yet, was trying to
cut back. This was before we
almost got the gas cut off, before
we lost electricity the first of
many times. After Justine had
been bullied out with her three
cats but Kristen—whom we
suspected was asexual and not
really lesbian—was still hanging
on even though she adopted yet
another cat into the loft without
asking. It was only one more,
she reasoned, but we already
had Seether, Amber, Balzac,
Gigli, and now Eva Luna.
Anna and Jackie came by,
they were friendly to me, but
Tjet and Julie weren't. T and J
were Clit Club. A and J were
literary. Then Michelle and
Shigi secretly slept together,
a disaster, and Cynthia got
kicked out for being bi and
then bringing a guy to the loft,
but that summer before all that,
just after I'd been dumped by
the girl I'd moved to NYC
to be with, and just after I'd
invited my first college girl-
friend to come visit me
(not sure what I expected
but she was the only one
who was willing to fly out)
but before I met Natira.
Our month-long affair
wasn't great but still pretty
damn good, she was the only
one I'd liked in a long time. I
hadn't met Sayeeda yet, at

Jackie's book party—Jackie
and Anna I think were broken
up by then. After Stefanie
but long before Tina, before
Jamie had even met Tina,
this song played everywhere,
every day, ceaselessly, so it
started to seem that *we* were
Melissa, that Cassandra,
foretelling in a ragged voice:
*"And I'm the only one who'll
drown in my desire for you."*
We meant that we too were
willing to do anything to
prove we were the only one
for someone that one summer.

from *The Literary Review*

Maid Maleen

◊   ◊   ◊

After seven years of damp walls, entombed, no more food,
she and her servant knife their way through the stone tower.
Their first glance outside, a shock. All has changed.
The country's burned and smashed, the banners rent.
No one alive in the castle or village, the farms just soot.
No alarms warned them: abandoned by her own father,
the king who walled his daughter up and forgot.

Eventually, the tale will be made right again.
A prince will fall in love with Maid Maleen, she will prosper
in her gold necklace and never want for food or home.

Rip out the last pages. There will be no wedding today.
The sulfurous fields don't lead to paths or healing rivers.
Never safety again. Once the smoke's in one's lungs,
it remains forever. The charred trees. The murdered bodies.

from *Harvard Review*

Grief

◇   ◇   ◇

Let it be seeds.
Let it be the slow tornado of seeds from the oak tree
by the gates to the playground in May wind.
Today is Mother's Day and someone said it is almost impossible
to remember something before you know the word for it
and the babies in their mothers' arms
stare at the seeds and they don't know
the word for falling. Nor the word for sudden or whirling.
Let it be something that doesn't last, not the moon.
Let it not be the rooftops that are so quiet.
Let it come to the white doorstep like rain and slide
onto the sidewalk not knowing. What is gentle if not time
but it's not time that is gentle, what will happen in the future
does not matter. Cicadas underground are called nymphs
and their wings look like tree seeds. Trapped under skin
and as soft as the dirt that surrounds them.
Teneral is a word for the days between
when the cicada digs its way out of earth and begins to sing
and when its self and shell are still
a single, susceptible thing. It is impossible
to remember. Let it be the years
underground, molting nymph skin
and moving in the soil without sound.
It's not time that is gentle but what unknown sign,
a method of counting each spring through the roots of a tree.
How they learn from the taste of a root's juice the moment
when in one rush they should push up to earth.
Teneral, meaning not yet hardened, a sense before a memory
of the shell. Let it be the sign in the cells

of the blind safe skin, the limbo of gold
walling here and there, where the baby waits
between a mother's body and the air's tears, he came
to my breast and rested, there was no before.
Let it be the gold room with its lack of door, that time
of day, cicadas will wait until sunset to break through the dirt.
Where did he go while I pushed?
We stood in the tunnel of seeds, windmills, a tree
had come to make promises. Rain to stone, rain to street.
They seemed while they fell to be lifting and we waited, watching,
the baby without words for what we were seeing.
Seeds pushing roots, brick, and dirt don't say
what they know about time. Rise. For days the whole town will sing.

from *The Massachusetts Review*

TOM SLEIGH

Prayer for Recovery

◇   ◇   ◇

The cursor moving back along the line erases what was was.
What was keeps existing under Edit so that all you need to do is
click Undo. So much of time gets lived out that way—
at the momentary center of the line erasing.

When I push my IV pole down the dark, glass hall, the droplets'
atavistic sheen drips into my veins with an absolute weight as if
the bag of potassium chloride, hanging in sovereign judgment
above my head, assures me that justice, death or life,

will be done. And though it's not for me to understand,
when I cross the beam that throws open the door so silently
and swiftly, it makes me want to think that like these rivets fastening

glass to iron, some state of me that was will go on,
either as the will of some will that isn't mine, or out of mercy,
or from the contract between the rivet gun and some unseen hand.

from *Raritan*

Alice, Bewildered

◊   ◊   ◊

Deep in the wood where things escape their names,
Her childish arm draped round the fawn's soft neck
(Her diffidence, its skittishness in check,
Merged in the anonymity that tames),
She knits her brow, but nothing now reclaims
The syllables that meant herself. Ah well,
She need not answer to the grown-up beck
And call, the rote-learned lessons, scolds and blames
Of girlhood, sentences to parse and gloss;
She's un-twinned from the likeness in the glass.
Yet in the dark ellipsis she can tell,
She's certain, that her name begins with "L"—
Liza, Lacie? Alias, alas,
A lass alike alone and at a loss.

from *Virginia Quarterly Review*

Cotton You Lose in the Field

◇   ◇   ◇

Some bad whiskey
I drink by myself
just like you
when this wind
blows as it does
in the delta
where a lost hearing aid
can be taken
for a grub worm
when the black constellations
make you swim backwards
in circles of blood
stableboys ruin their hands
for a while
and a man none of us
can do without
breaks his neck
jumping over some hill
chasing the fox
of a half-pint
and a fine-blooded horse
is put out of its misery
even the young sisters
of the boys we run with
we would give our fingers
to touch them again
but this war

seeps back into us
little insecticide
and the white cricket of those days
drags itself off the hook
there are no more fish
there is no more bait
the rivers are formed by the tears of sports fans
we try to pour a trail of salt
as if making a long fuse
with a gunpowder keg
we try to swim away from the gym
like slugs with gills
the girls from the other school
step off the bus
the clouds are weighed in at the gin
there is a pattern to all this
like a weave of a skirt
we all go crazy from looking

from Poem-a-Day

SUSAN STEWART

What Piranesi Knew

◊   ◊   ◊

          as he drew the silhouettes
against the vast
                    machinery, suspending them,
                    haggard, bent
in a direction that was not
          a direction,
for the stairs and bridges, ladders and catwalks
swaying
          over danger,
          over chasm and
damage, had in truth
no exit or entry.
                    Those beings embodied
                              the thrown existence
of the living in an iron world.

Who, then, can say we should lift
                    our faces to the light's
                    slow filter,
and trace the funnel back to its fiery
                    source and be
                    glad, and be glad?

          from *The Paris Review*

Drones: An Exercise in Awe-Terror

◊   ◊   ◊

Pilot, Creech Air Force Base; Indian Springs, Nevada

I. The Imagination Cannot

A sea of, a drowning of—everything seems
to be red rock. Prickling of dust and salt.
Seething, the sun between
the shrubs.

Rocks are pocked with
gorges to the core. Something
bad in there, in each
one, every cave caves into
more caves than seconds
in which a man can yes
can die. They

told me there's a place like
that, and I am actually in
it (changing
it) (right now)

II. When Reason Came

Across this gray terrain: North
South East West. "Your enemy

doesn't wear a uniform. Find him. Find
his patterns of life. There's no place

in this country where we cannot see him."
There are two men, carrying
guns. Adjust the crosshair above
the bodies. Fifteen seconds. Five

four three two one
zero. White fire
opens a seam in the map.
We nicknamed our eye in the sky

the Gorgon stare. I stare there,
right there: It turns
to a perfect not-
there.

III. Black

      Walking through the park in Indian Springs. Watching
TV about what they did.

     (When the rocks turn black: it has happened.)

     Watching reflections
in the cloudy glass   Liquefying

                 completely, like spring
                 snow like expiring
                 during sex.

(Rocks turning black: it has happened.)

Dreaming of those who hide
in caves. Watching TV about what they
did.

(The heart's cavity held stone and clear, cold lakes)

Surely, the people wanted

(Lock up the target. Spin up
the weapon.)

Blacken did
the shrubs, the ridged
rock. Black go
Nevada

from *Tahoma Literary Review*

Peaches

◇　◇　◇

A crate of peaches straight from the farm
has to be maintained, or eaten in days.
Obvious, but in my family, they went so fast,
I never saw the mess that punishes delay.

I thought everyone bought fruit by the crate,
stored it in the coolest part of the house,
then devoured it before any could rot.
I'm from the Peach State, and to those

who ask *But where are you from originally*,
I'd like to reply *The homeland of the peach*,
but I'm too nice, and they might not look it up.
In truth, the reason we bought so much

did have to do with being Chinese—at least
Chinese in that part of America, both strangers
and natives on a lonely, beautiful street
where food came in stackable containers

and fussy bags, unless you bothered to drive
to the source, where the same money landed
a bushel of fruit, a twenty-pound sack of rice.
You had to drive anyway, each house surrounded

by land enough to grow your own, if lawns
hadn't been required. At home I loved to stare
into the extra freezer, reviewing mountains
of foil-wrapped meats, cakes, juice concentrate,

mysterious packets brought by houseguests
from New York Chinatown, to be transformed
by heat, force, and my mother's patient effort,
enough to keep us fed through flood or storm,

provided the power stayed on, or fire and ice
could be procured, which would be labor-intensive,
but so was everything else my parents did.
Their lives were labor, they kept this from the kids,

who grew up to confuse work with pleasure,
to become typical immigrants' children,
taller than their parents and unaware of hunger
except when asked the odd, perplexing question.

from Poem-a-Day

Dome of
the Hidden Temple

◇ ◇ ◇

People were going about their chores. Some were eating
lunch. Others, like me, were just standing around doing nothing,
just taking in the scene. I saw a dozen ducks fly over low
on their way to the pond. A policeman walked by swinging his
club. The firemen were washing their fire truck. Margie walked
out of a shoe store and saw me. She walked up to me and said,
"Have you heard the news? Rosie and Larry broke up." "Why?
They were the best darn couple I knew," I said. "I agree.
They had everything going for them," she said. "Did you talk
to her?" I said. "She said he thinks he's an armadillo. He
eats insects and mud and dug a burrow in the back of the house,"
she said. "He didn't look like an armadillo. I thought he was
a very good-looking guy, always very nice to me," I said. "Whatever
the case, I'll miss their parties. They were always such fun,"
she said. "They were the best," I said. "I've got to run, nice
to see you, Tim," she said. I walked over to the drugstore and
bought myself some toothpaste. When I came out, a light spring
rain had started. The pigeons on the bank took off and flew in
circles around the town. A man walked up to me and said, "Do
you know where the Dome of the Hidden Temple is?" I said, "Yes,
but I can't tell you. It's a secret." "But I'm supposed to meet
somebody there," he said. "Then that person should have told
you how to get there," I said. "I guess he thought I knew," he
said. "Almost nobody knows," I said. "Then why do you know?"
he said. "Because I am the Priest of Nothingness," I said.

"Are you really?" he said. "No, I just made that up," I said. "Oh, so you're a comedian," he said. "Yes, I'm a comedian," I said. "Well, you're not very good," he said. "I know," I said.

from *jubilat*

LEE UPTON

The Apology

◇　◇　◇

Tonight outside the plate glass
each insect is made of a long tube of wood,
as if the insect had become a tree
to give the tree a voice.
And these pink spatters,
these crumbled parlor doilies,
these milkweed blossoms
fade as if antique,
and the milkweed does not report on the condition of its leaves,
the height of its flowers,
its life without bureaucracy,
nor does the lilac filtering the mentholated air,
or the bee drowsing on the sill
after straining through the broken window screen
like Rilke wheedling his way into a palace.
Or the brook that runs by the cabin
talking nonsense.
Or the willow that slouches as if it were in a classroom
where the teacher bores it.
So forgive me please already.
I am sorry for speaking for nature.
But it was asking for it.

from *The New Yorker*

C . K . W I L L I A M S

Hog

◊   ◊   ◊

In a certain town in New Jersey where now will be found malls car
     dealerships drive-throughs
highways with synchronized lights a motor-vehicle office a store
     selling discount something or other
I can't remember what else but haven't we all experienced such post-
     agrarian transmogrifications

In a certain town in New Jersey once was a farm farmed by a Jewish
     farmer a *Jewish farmer*
my goodness a notion I'd never entertained Jews were lawyers
     accountants doctors maybe salesmen
until a friend took me to meet one his uncle his mother's brother who
     lived somewhere I'd never heard of

In a certain town in New Jersey not far from where I am now existed a
     farmer who was also a Jew
who'd eluded the second war murders by leaving for the States with
     nothing in his wallet or satchel
but a hammer and saw and a handful of nails and worked his way
     through the shit-pit of Europe to here

where he went back with somebody else's money some earlier escapee-
     arrival's maybe his sister's
to farming which had been his family's trade for many generations in
     the old country he boasted
and there he was on his farm now with his chickens and corn and I
     saw three or four cows and some pigs

and on this day a dead hog that is to say a hog he'd only just slaughtered
      that hung upside down
from a hook in a rafter and a stout iron chain and which the farmer
      the Jewish farmer was flinging
boiling water against flinging and flinging so its bristles would soften
      which I could see they had

for then he was scraping the hog with a crescent-shaped length of steel
      and the bristles were loosening
and I gathered that when they were gone he'd be (how had the word
      ever found me) *gutting* the hog
there was a gleaming well-honed knife at the ready whose task I could
      tell was slicing you open

as you horribly swung there colorless gunk spooling out of your snout
      while the booted farmer
methodically effected the everlasting labor of farmers Jewish or not
      pulling you with his knotty arms
and leather gloves towards him to cut you apart and sell you I
      supposed is what would come next

In a certain town in New Jersey might anyone remain to ask
      forgiveness for the concrete and asphalt
the forests felled for McMansions the eternally lost corn and wheat
      fields and vanished orchards
might anyone recall the sweet stink of manure of tilled earth the odor
      even of fresh blood on a floor

and who besides me will remember the farmer so imposing in the
      masterful exercise of his calling
who with a snort and a clap on the back forgave me the gawk of my
      adolescence as imagining
the rest of what life would be bringing I knelt by a rusting soon to be
      scrapped hay rake and threw up

from *The New Yorker*

ELEANOR WILNER

To Think
of How Cold

◊　◊　◊

Cold in the earth—and the deep snow piled above thee
　　　　　—Emily Brontë, "Remembrance"

To think of how cold in the earth—how cold
　　　to have let her bury him, wrong, wrong, wrong . . .
　　　　　　wrong says the struck bell, the footsteps of bronze,
wrong says the path through echoing stones,
　　　wrong says the cypress, casting a long
　　　　　　Tuscan shadow on Ohio ground, all wrong
to let him lie below the lawn where no one walks
　　　with a light step, or a lifted heart—no one,
　　　　　　no one—the hawthorn trees are skeletal,
only the pines offer shelter to the silent wren,
　　　but the bird has forgotten everything, its song, even
　　　　　　the shape of its nest, and the rest of it—
it paused too long on an angel of stone, only
　　　those marble wings could bear the cold here;
　　　　　　cold in the earth—you imagine a room
carved from icy clay, roots dangling from its roof,
　　　feeding a tree that he cannot see
　　　　　　from geometry's hollow under the snow,
and cold, so implacably cold. *Do not grow old,*
　　　as I grew old, says the ghost of Lear, *for though*
　　　　　　I am gone, and the stage grown dark,
I walk the heath and my mind conjures
　　　an end to this cold, a funeral pyre—and look! Cordelia

145

coming at last, like a blazing torch,
in a heaven of heat and a roar of fire.

from *New Ohio Review*

AL YOUNG

The Drummer Omar: Poet of Percussion

◊ ◊ ◊

Rhythm is the prime element of music—music is life.
—Omar Clay

In memory of Omar Clay (1935–2008)

We met when it was spring, before the heat
of life moved in. We met before blue summer
got us up running, racing to some beat
we couldn't count on or off. You peeped it, Omar.

You showed up everyplace I turned—New York,
The Showcase, Mingus, Oakland, midnights, dawn.
You and Bob James: a silver spoon and fork
to match the knife-shy hush of Sarah Vaughan.

You aired the groove. Yes, you, Omar, you drew
all space between the beat into your lungs
in micro-breaths. All tempo burned in you.
"Omar," it cried, "hear how my silence sings!"

We'll meet again, I know. You loved to teach.
You'll show me rhythm time can never touch.

from *Brilliant Corners*

CONTRIBUTORS' NOTES AND COMMENTS

CHRISTOPHER BAKKEN was born in Madison, Wisconsin, in 1967. He is the author of three books of poetry: *Eternity & Oranges* (Pitt Poetry Series, 2016), *Goat Funeral* (Sheep Meadow, 2006), and *After Greece* (Truman State University Press, 2001). He has also written a book of travel writing, *Honey, Olives, Octopus: Adventures at the Greek Table* (University of California Press, 2013), and he is cotranslator of *The Lions' Gate: Selected Poems of Titos Patrikios* (Truman State UP, 2006). A former Fulbright Scholar at the University of Bucharest, he teaches at Allegheny College and is director of Writing Workshops in Greece: Thessaloniki and Thasos.

Of "Sentence," Bakken writes: "This poem was written during a very cold night at the Virginia Center for the Creative Arts. An ice storm arrived during my residency and the power went out—so we had no heat. I could see my breath inside my little studio, but words were coming to me and so I stayed put, layering on every item of clothing I had with me, and writing by flashlight at night. I'd been thinking about Greece, as I almost always am, specifically about the winters there, when tourists depart, and the rhythms of life and labor slow almost to a halt, and the Greeks are left to themselves.

"The encounter described in the poem was in part remembered from the winter of 1993, when I lived in Thessaloniki, a beautiful, haunted city, in the final decade of a brutal century—one that had brought to Thessaloniki the devastations of the Holocaust, not to mention more recent outbursts of xenophobia and violence. Just a few hours north, war was raging in a place that had once been called Yugoslavia.

"As the poem's long, single sentence gathered momentum, bringing new things to bear upon the scene, the frozen priest arrived and I let him thaw."

CATHERINE BARNETT is the author of *The Game of Boxes* (Graywolf Press, 2012) and *Into Perfect Spheres Such Holes Are Pierced* (Alice James Books, 2004). She teaches at New York University, is a visiting professor in the Hunter College MFA program, and works as an independent editor. She has degrees from Princeton University, where she has taught in the Lewis Center for the Arts, and from the MFA Program for Writers at Warren Wilson College. She has received a James Laughlin Award, a Guggenheim Fellowship, and a Whiting Writers' Award.

Barnett writes: "Although I often think things are heading in the wrong direction, underneath I am what some people have called an enigmatic optimist. ('Chronically hopeful,' someone once said.) 'O Esperanza!' is a revision of several actual and imagined facts. I wrote the poem right after having had the good fortune to attend a three-hour clown class (who knew such a thing existed?) with the spectacular Sarah French. I'd been told that Sarah would simply lay a rope down on the floor and all we'd have to do to become a clown was step over it. I wanted to try it because I wanted to perform without performing. Something to do with Being and Time, I imagine. It was one of the most difficult classes I've attended, which made me think of the philosopher Richard Rorty's afternoon lectures, difficult in mostly very different ways. I was thrilled to discover his quote and wished I'd been able to understand more of what he was saying while he was standing right before my eyes. Like so many other poets, I've been well nourished on confusion and hope, both. And I have a habit of counting syllables (12 or 285 or 308, depending where you start and/or end)."

RICK BAROT was born in the Philippines in 1969. He has published three books of poetry with Sarabande Books: *The Darker Fall* (2002), *Want* (2008), and *Chord* (2015). He lives in Tacoma, Washington, and directs the Rainier Writing Workshop, the low-residency MFA program at Pacific Lutheran University. He is the poetry editor of *New England Review*.

Barot writes: "I came across the story recounted in 'Whitman, 1841' in David S. Reynolds's terrific book, *Walt Whitman's America: A Cultural Biography*. Did the incident actually happen? Reynolds presents some riveting evidence that says so."

JILL BIALOSKY was born in Cleveland, Ohio. She received her BA from Ohio University, an MA from the Johns Hopkins University, and an MFA from the University of Iowa Writers' Workshop. She has written three novels: *House Under Snow* (Houghton Mifflin Harcourt, 2002), *The Life Room* (Harcourt, 2007), and *The Prize* (Counterpoint Press, 2015). Her four volumes of poetry are *The End of Desire* (Alfred A. Knopf, 1997), *Subterranean* (Knopf, 2007), *Intruder* (Knopf, 2010), and *The Players* (Knopf, 2015). She is the author of a memoir, *History of a Suicide: My Sister's Unfinished Life* (Atria Books, 2011). She is coeditor, with Helen Schulman, of *Wanting a Child* (Farrar, Straus and Giroux, 1999). She lives in New York City.

Of "Daylight Savings," Bialosky writes: "This poem was inspired by the first November afternoon after we've turned back the clocks and leave our offices to the shock of darkness. I began to ponder the idea of time passing and what is lost in that hour and of course, what we cherish."

PAULA BOHINCE was born in Pennsylvania in 1976. Her three poetry collections are from Sarabande Books: *Swallows and Waves* (2016), *The Children* (2012), and *Incident at the Edge of Bayonet Woods* (2008). She has received a fellowship from the National Endowment for the Arts and the Amy Lowell Poetry Traveling Scholarship as well as awards from the Poetry Society of America and the United Kingdom National Poetry Competition. She lives with her husband in Pennsylvania.

Bohince writes: "When I lived in Paris, I went on long walks and filled my eyes and notebooks with images from art and everyday life. The ones in 'Fruits de Mer' rested in mind for several years before they rose to the surface in a low-key castle in Scotland, the poem then revised with good suggestions from Herbert Leibowitz, editor of *Parnassus*. The imagined feast in Hemingway's La Closerie des Lilas seemed more crucial each time I visited it: the ambivalence in the luxurious meal against lines that hold so much death. The *Le Monde* headline translates to 'Justice is served.' This poem, in its push-pull of war and hope, to me seems mostly about the power of images and imagination, wedding the visible and invisible."

MICHELLE BOISSEAU was born in Cincinnati, Ohio, in 1955. She teaches in the MFA program at the University of Missouri–Kansas City, where she is senior editor of BkMk Press and a contributing editor of *New Letters*. She won the Tampa Review Prize for her fifth book of poems, *Among the Gorgons* (Tampa Review Press, 2016). *A Sunday in God-Years* (University of Arkansas Press, 2009) examines her paternal ancestors' slave-holding past in Virginia into the seventeenth century. Other titles include *Trembling Air* (University of Arkansas Press, 2003), *Understory* (Northeastern University Press, 1996), and *No Private Life* (Vanderbilt University Press, 1990). The eighth edition of her textbook, *Writing Poems* (Longman Publishing Group), was written collaboratively with Hadara Bar-Nadav. Boisseau has received two fellowships from the National Endowment for the Arts.

Boisseau writes: "Over the past several years, as I worked on the poems that became *Among the Gorgons*, I have been exploring the double helix of the beautiful and the monstrous. As I was thinking about an incident between two of the giants of literature, 'Ugglig' came to be."

MARIANNE BORUCH, a native of Chicago, passed through its parish schools, then the University of Illinois at Urbana, and finally the University of Massachusetts, where she received her MFA in 1979. Her eighth poetry collection, *Cadaver, Speak*, came out in 2014 from Copper Canyon Press, which will publish her *Eventually One Dreams the Real Thing* in 2016. *The Book of Hours* (2011), from the same publisher, won the 2013 Kingsley Tufts Poetry Award. Her prose includes two essay collections on poetry, *Poetry's Old Air* (University of Michigan Press, 1995) and *In the Blue Pharmacy* (Trinity University Press, 2005), and a memoir, *The Glimpse Traveler* (Indiana University Press, 2011). A former Guggenheim Fellow, she was a 2012 Fulbright/Visiting Professor at the University of Edinburgh and a resident at the Rockefeller Foundation's Bellagio Center. She teaches at Purdue University and in the low-residency MFA Program at Warren Wilson College.

Of "I Get to Float Invisible," Boruch writes: "A lot of time is spent overhearing things. Shards and hesitations and curious claims. I stumbled into this fractured real story by accident, the brother of the woman in question arguing how impressive his sister's poems about adultery were. Adultery! I was a stranger. No matter. But words *mean* and follow you.

"And images haunt: her brother's blithe retelling in public, the young woman drinking alone, writing such things as her world breaks around her. Maybe I was merely picking up the soundtrack of what it is to live with so little privacy now, taking in intimacies we have no right to know, engaged in an empathy strange and compelling, often out of the nowhere of subway cars and elevators and grocery lines. People move, hold forth, rage and love and shrug while we let a world fall through us. And some of it catches."

DAVID BOTTOMS was born in Canton, Georgia, in 1949. His first book, *Shooting Rats at the Bibb County Dump*, was chosen by Robert Penn Warren as winner of the 1979 Walt Whitman Award of the Academy of American Poets. He is the author of eight books of poetry, two novels, and a book of essays and interviews. His most recent book of poems, *We Almost Disappear*, was released in fall 2011 by Copper Canyon Press. He has held appointments at the University of Montana, Mercer University, Johns Hopkins University, and Georgia Tech, and teaches at the Sarah Lawrence Summer Writing Seminars. He served for twelve years as poet laureate of Georgia. He is a member of the Georgia Writers Hall of Fame and a founding editor of *Five Points: A Journal of Literature & Art*. He lives with his wife and daughter in Atlanta, where he holds the Amos Distinguished Chair in English Letters at Georgia State University.

Of "Hubert Blankenship," Bottoms writes: "For a little more than fifty years, my grandfather ran a country store in Canton, Georgia. He sold mostly canned goods, but also an assortment of things ranging from horse feed to fishing lures. Most of his customers were very much like Hubert Blankenship, poor but proud. They were hardworking dirt farmers and cotton mill hands."

JOSEPH CHAPMAN was born in Charlotte, North Carolina, in 1982. He studied English, philosophy, and creative writing at the University of North Carolina at Chapel Hill and went on to earn an MFA in poetry at the University of Virginia. His work was chosen for *The Best American Poetry 2012*. He is currently in the first year of a master of divinity program at San Francisco Theological Seminary.

Of "32 Fantasy Football Teams," Chapman writes: "It may seem bold to start off an artist's statement with self-congratulations, but rereading this poem I'm struck by just how plain funny and alive it is. That probably shouldn't have been the case. When George David Clark, a good friend from my MFA days and the editor of *32 Poems*, solicited a list poem from me, I knew I needed to collaborate with someone if I was going to write anything resembling humorous poetry. The thing is, I didn't feel up to writing a playful poem on my own—my own poems were stalled, I felt stalled at my desk job—and so I selfishly got in touch with someone whose energy would be catching. Laura Eve [Engel], with whom I co-taught at the Young Writers Workshop at the University of Virginia and who is also one of the funniest people I know, agreed to collaborate with me. It took only one or two emails to settle on our title. The puns came pretty quickly after that, as did the last line. It was a blast to write. In 'The Figure a Poem Makes' Robert Frost famously cautions poets, 'No tears in the writer, no tears in the reader.' However, this collaborative poem reminded me of the simple delight of wordplay. It reminded me that if I'm not having fun then the reader probably isn't either."

See Laura Eve Engel, coauthor of "32 Fantasy Football Teams," in these Contributors' Notes.

MICHAEL COLLIER was born in Phoenix, Arizona, in 1953. His two most recent collections of poetry are *Dark Wild Realm* (Houghton Mifflin, 2006) and *An Individual History* (W. W. Norton, 2012). He teaches at the University of Maryland and is the director of the Bread Loaf Writers' Conference.

Of "Last Morning with Steve Orlen," Collier writes: "A few days before Steve Orlen passed away, on November 16, 2010, a little less than three weeks after having been diagnosed with lung cancer, he told his wife, Gail, that he'd never been happier in his life. He had spent the afternoon in his backyard, stretched out on a bed in full pasha mode, visiting with friends, talking about poetry and art, gossiping, telling stories, and offering up semi-oracular statements. Although he hadn't eaten for several days, when a friend showed up with a loaf of home-made challah, Steve ate hunks of it slathered with butter and fig jam. I was fortunate to be there, among his friends, and he did seem truly happy. He was also fearless, and the way he faced death inspired and encouraged those who were with him. It's not surprising that he was happy; friendship was one of the most abiding forces in his life.

"I met Steve in 1975 through John Murphy, my closest high school friend from Phoenix, who was taking undergraduate creative writing classes from him at the University of Arizona. Two years later, I entered the MFA program at Arizona, where I spent two important years studying with Steve. Not only did he have tremendous influence on the way I wrote poems, but his generosity and openness as a person were a model of affectionate friendship. He was also wonderfully irreverent and loved letting the air out of pretentious behavior, real or perceived. One of his missions with me was to wear off what he thought was a sheen I had picked up by going east to Connecticut College, where I had been a student of William Meredith's. This is how he chided me about my woeful condition, in a 1976 letter: 'Tho you do have some polish & a bit of manners, you're still just a regular asshole from Phoenix, and your poetry stuff should reflect it.'

"In 1999, a few weeks before we were to teach together at Warren Wilson College, Steve sent me a letter in which he described the importance of having 'at least one "intimate" friend to pal around with' during the residency, so that 'every once in a while' they could 'get deeper into friendship.' He offered this as an example of that 'deeper friendship': 'One late night, last residency with Tony [Hoagland], and I'm in my chair and he's sitting cross-legged on my bed in his long johns, on his head, a bright yellow T-shirt tied up to stay put, not like an Arab headdress, but like a—what?—a clown hat, or something. I laughed at him, and he said in his defining, factual, defending, self-laughing way, that bald people lose most of their body heat through their heads. I tell you, I love friendship almost more than anything in life.'

"'Last Morning with Steve Orlen' follows pretty closely the visit of the final morning I had with Steve. The day before, I'd heard Gail say she was trying to find a way to go to the gym, to get out of the house for a bit, so we agreed that since I wake early and was staying with Buzz and Linda Poverman a few blocks away, I'd come over at 7 a.m. She thought Steve would likely be asleep and all I'd need to do was be in the house in case he woke, but when I arrived and just as I was about to ring the doorbell, I could hear Gail laughing and Steve chuckling in his distinctive, resonant way, so I opened the door on my own, called out, and followed their voices to Steve's study, which had been set up as his sickroom. Gail was sitting at the middle of the bed and Steve was propped up at the head. It was clear that whatever Steve had been saying to Gail had delighted her and probably even embarrassed her, which is something he liked to do. I asked Steve, perfunctorily, how he'd slept, and then he launched into the business of writing the novel, English or Russian. The 'faithful amanuensis' refers to the fact that over the past few days when Steve would say something he was particularly proud of, that seemed to have poetic possibilities, he would ask whoever was near to write it down, and by the same token if you said something he liked, he'd want you to add it as well to the notebook being kept for his utterances. I wish I could serve up one or two of these mostly surreal bon mots, but I can't, although you get a sense of what they were like in Steve's morning claim that he'd spent the night in serious literary endeavor, fueled by terminal morphine."

ALLISON PITINII DAVIS was born in Youngstown, Ohio, in 1986. She received an MFA from Ohio State University and received fellowships from the Fine Arts Work Center in Provincetown, the Wallace Stegner Program at Stanford University, and the Severinghaus Beck Fund for Study at Vilnius Yiddish Institute. She is the author of *Poppy Seeds* (Kent State University Press, 2013) and a forthcoming book (tentatively titled *Line Study of a Motel Clerk*) from Baobab Press in 2017.

Of "The Heart of It All + A Free Beer," Davis writes: " 'The Heart of It All' was the slogan on Ohio license plates. The poem would be funny if it wasn't difficult getting dumped so many times. It's a companion to my poem 'Falls In Love, Or Reads Spinoza,' in which I'm rejected by this poem's Lorca translator. I grew up in a family that runs a motel and I helped clean rooms, so my early encounters with love was after it was over, the crumpled sheets left behind. Somewhat like when I swept theaters after movies, that sense of entering a room as everyone else is leaving it. This is the moment of this poem's narration—I walk into the poem after all these failed relationships expecting abandoned space. But then I run into family members, into history, into the sense—to badly paraphrase Brodsky—that we're effects trying to reconstruct a cause. My parents, who wait for each other at the end of the poem, are happily married. I've since found love as well."

OLENA KALYTIAK DAVIS was born Ukrainian in Detroit in 1963. She "engages in the practice of law and, way more rarely, poetry, in the Detroit-like Anchorage, Alaska. Check out the review of *The Poem She Didn't Write and Other Poems* (Copper Canyon Press, 2014) in *The New Yorker*. It was very good."

Of "On the Certainty of Bryan," Kalytiak Davis writes: "In a spirit of collaboration/testing, I asked my friend Bryan, who stars in the poem to edit the poem. He was audacious (maybe not but yes and yes), and/but oddly sparing and accurate, so I decided to keep and highlight his edits (ideally they should/would be red). I did invent the 'endless line' all by myself, if that is an invention. The 'issue with the tongue on/through the front' is an issue of *Green Mountains Review*. The Glück poem is 'An Adventure.' Bryan has recently quit his job."

NATALIE DIAZ was born and raised in the Fort Mojave Indian Village in Needles, California, on the banks of the Colorado River. She is Mojave and an enrolled member of the Gila River Indian Tribe. Her first poetry collection, *When My Brother Was an Aztec*, was published by Copper

Canyon Press in 2012. She is a Lannan Literary Fellow and a Native Arts Council Foundation Artist Fellow. She was awarded a Bread Loaf Fellowship, the Holmes National Poetry Prize, a Hodder Fellowship, and a PEN/Civitella Ranieri Foundation Residency. She teaches at the Institute of American Indian Arts Low Rez MFA program and splits her time between the East Coast and Mohave Valley, Arizona, where she works to revitalize the Mojave language.

Of "How the Milky Way Was Made," Diaz writes: "This poem speaks to specific beasts of me—coyotes and the mythical salmon of my Mojave desert. *'Achii 'ahan* translates to *the true fish*, because they were so revered by my people. Though they are not related to salmon, they were as resilient, leaping puddle to puddle after rains, flipping themselves across the desert, escaping lagoons after spring floods. Like me, like all my beasts, they have teeth. They are endangered, as is their home—the Colorado River is the most endangered river in the United States. In the Mojave sky, there is no man in the moon—we see Coyote, who tripped and fell into the moon when he tried to steal a fish as they leapt the night. We call the Milky Way *the road the true fish make across the sky.* As it is every time I follow the beasts of hunger and teeth to the page into the night, I am led to my own desires."

DENISE DUHAMEL was born in Providence, Rhode Island, in 1961. Her most recent book of poetry, *Blowout* (University of Pittsburgh Press, 2013), won the 2014 Paterson Poetry Prize. Her other books include *Ka-Ching!* (Pittsburgh, 2009), *Two and Two* (Pittsburgh, 2005), *Queen for a Day: Selected and New Poems* (Pittsburgh, 2001), *The Star-Spangled Banner* (winner of the Crab Orchard Award; Southern Illinois University Press, 1999), and *Kinky* (Orchises Press, 1997). In 2015 Sibling Rivalry Press published *CAPRICE: (Collaborations: Collected, Uncollected, and New)*, a retrospective of her work with Maureen Seaton. She has received fellowships from the Guggenheim Foundation and the National Endowment for the Arts. She was the guest editor for *The Best American Poetry 2013* and is a professor at Florida International University in Miami.

Of "Humanity 101," Duhamel writes: "This poem started with a Words with Friends game in which I added an E to 'HUMAN' so I could branch out to a triple word score. The big difference between being human and humane haunted me, as sometimes words within words do. When I started thinking of humanity and the humanities, I was off to the poetry races. My smartphone guilty pleasure has led me to build the word 'WOMEN' from 'OMEN,' another unsettling poetry-producing moment."

LYNN EMANUEL (born 1949, Mt. Kisco, New York) is the author of five books of poetry: *Hotel Fiesta* (University of Georgia Press, 1984), *The Dig* (University of Illinois Press, 1992), *Then, Suddenly*—(University of Pittsburgh Poetry Series, 1999), *Noose and Hook* (University of Pittsburgh Poetry Series, 2010), and, most recently, *The Nerve of It: Poems New and Selected* (University of Pittsburgh Poetry Series, 2015). Her work has been featured in *The Pushcart Prize Anthology* and *The Best American Poetry* and is included in *The Oxford Book of American Poetry* and the Norton anthology of American hybrid poetry. She has taught at the Bread Loaf Writers' Conference, the Warren Wilson program in creative writing, and the Bennington College low-residency program. She has received two fellowships from the National Endowment for the Arts, the National Poetry Series Award, the Eric Matthieu King Award from the Academy of American Poets, and, most recently, a fellowship residency at the Civitella Ranieri Foundation in Umbria.

Emanuel writes: "'My Life' is adapted from the Middle English alliterative poem *Patience* (*Pacience*) written by the poet variously known as the 'Pearl' or 'Gawain' poet. *Patience* narrates the Old Testament story of how Jonas (as he is called in the poem) tests God's patience, is swallowed by the whale, and is then released. The poem is a fairly straightforward telling of the story, but there are important differences between the Bible's manner of presiding over that story and the poem's. First, there is the colloquial tone Jonas uses to address God and, second, there are the extraordinary descriptions and images. One of the most famous (Jonas entering the mouth of the whale like a mote of dust entering the door of a cathedral) I kept intact, although adapted for my own purposes. I also preserved two Middle English words because I could not translate them without losing their power. The first of these is 'muckle,' from which we get 'much,' but which in Middle English means 'enormous' or 'huge.' The second is 'bower.' In Middle English this simply means 'room.'"

CLAUDIA EMERSON (1957–2014) was raised in Chatham, Virginia. She wrote five books of poetry and taught creative writing at Virginia Commonwealth University in Richmond, Virginia, from 2012 until her death in 2014. A Guggenheim Fellow, she won the Pulitzer Prize for poetry for her third collection of poems, *Late Wife*, and was appointed poet laureate of Virginia in 2008. *Late Wife* (Louisiana State University, 2005) deals with her experience of falling in love with a man whose wife had succumbed to lung cancer. "When someone is missing, their possessions take on meaning," she said, echoing William Carlos Williams, who remarked that "one has emotions about the strangest things." Emerson also drew inspiration from her Southern background. She wrote country music. Of teaching writing at universities, she said, "If they were students of guitar, I would be insisting similarly that they learn guitar, not just a song or two. You need to know how to play the guitar before you smash it to pieces onstage. If you can't actually play, you're just a vandal."

In a 2013 interview with *Birmingham Poetry Review*, Emerson remarked: "I have long thought that the urge people have to photograph and video every experience is borne of that anxiety to stop time and somehow save it, or 'capture' it as though it were a wild animal. My lens happens to be language, the highly ordered language of poetry. It's a slow exposure, though, and a poem can take anywhere from days to years for me to bring it to its finest clarity." Also, "We share this planet with all sorts of creatures whom we as human beings tend to see as not just *other* but *lesser*, and I have long been concerned with what I saw even as a child as a disharmony with the greater natural world of which we are part, and from which we are apart."

LAURA EVE ENGEL has received fellowships from the Provincetown Fine Arts Work Center and the Wisconsin Institute for Creative Writing. She is the residential program director of the University of Virginia Young Writers Workshop.

See Joseph Chapman's note for a comment on the poem Chapman wrote in collaboration with Engel, "32 Fantasy Football Teams."

MARTÍN ESPADA was born in Brooklyn, New York, in 1957. He has published nearly twenty books as a poet, editor, essayist, and translator. His collections of poems include *Vivas to Those Who Have Failed* (W. W. Norton, 2016), *The Trouble Ball* (Norton, 2011), *The Republic of Poetry* (Norton, 2006), and *Alabanza* (Norton, 2003). He has received the Shelley Memorial Award, the Robert Creeley Award, and a Guggenheim Fellowship. His book of essays, *Zapata's Disciple* (South End, 1998), was banned in Tucson as part of the Mexican-American Studies Program outlawed by the state of Arizona. A former tenant lawyer, he is a professor of English at the University of Massachusetts–Amherst.

Of "Here I Am," Espada writes: "José 'JoeGo' Gouveia was a poet, cultural organizer, columnist, radio programmer, raconteur, and close friend. The son of Portuguese immigrants born in Taunton, Massachusetts, he lived many lives, from carpenter to biker, before earning an MFA from New England College. He had a genius for generosity. He served as the poetry curator at the Cultural Center of Cape Cod, wrote 'The Meter Man' poetry column for *The Barnstable Patriot* in Hyannis, and hosted the 'Poets' Corner' radio show on WOMR-FM in Provincetown. He also edited *Rubber Side Down: The Biker Poet Anthology* (Archer Books, 2008). Gouveia published one full-length collection of poems, *Saudades*, with Casa Mariposa Press. He died in May 2014 at age forty-nine, one month after his book was published."

PETER EVERWINE was born in Detroit in 1930 and raised in western Pennsylvania. He was educated at Northwestern University, U.S. Army (1952–54), University of Iowa, and Stanford. His most recent books are *From the Meadow: Selected and New Poems* (2004) and *Listening Long and Late* (2013), both from the University of Pittsburgh Press. *A Small Clearing* is forthcoming from Aureole Press. He has received fellowships from the National Endowment for the Arts and the Guggenheim Foundation and won an American Academy of Arts and Letters Award in Literature. He lives in Fresno, California.

Of "The Kiskiminetas River," Everwine writes: "My grandparents were immigrants from the Piedmont region in Italy. They settled in one of the small towns along the river in a valley rich in coal mines and mills. I grew up there, in households in which the old dialect was still spoken. I've written about my family in other places. But I wanted to write something about the river, since it was so much a part of that world. Like many industrial rivers, it was polluted and ugly, and later in life I would see many beautiful and famous rivers. None touched me as deeply, or more often, than the Kiskiminetas. I felt I needed to write about it, especially since humanity, in this century, seems to grow more and more homeless. The river remains, but that world I love will vanish when I do."

ALEXIS RHONE FANCHER is a lifelong Los Angeleno. She has a BA in theater from University of California at Santa Barbara. She is a professional photographer, and in her Los Angeles Poets Project she hopes to document more than two hundred Southern California poets. Her one-woman show at Beyond Baroque in April of 2015 featured the first thirty-five. Alexis is the author of *How I Lost My Virginity to Michael Cohen and other heart-stab poems* (Sybaritic Press, 2014), and *State of Grace: The Joshua Elegies* (KYSO Flash Press, 2015). Since 2012 she has been poetry editor of *Cultural Weekly*, where she also publishes a monthly photo-essay, "The Poet's Eye," which documents her continuing love affair with Los Angeles. You can hear her on her website, alexisrhonefancher.com.

Of "When I turned fourteen, my mother's sister took me to lunch and said:" Fancher writes: "Soon after the publication of my first book, *How I Lost My Virginity to Michael Cohen and other heart-stab poems*, the book's namesake, the *real* Michael Cohen, posted a review on Amazon. His words were complimentary. He gave the book five stars. His only complaint? He had 'friended' me on Facebook, and I had chosen to ignore him. He wrote that I might still be miffed over the 'Debbie episode,' when he'd slept with my younger sister. Only two years apart, Debbie and I were always competitive. Michael Cohen's words brought back my adolescence with a vengeance. I now have eight 'sister' poems, and counting.

"When Debbie read 'When I turned fourteen, my mother's sister took me to lunch and said:' in *Ragazine*, she shared with me *her* memories of those turbulent years. We reminisced for hours. It was the closest we've ever been."

CHARLES FORT was born in New Britain, Connecticut, in 1951. He taught at the University of Nebraska at Kearney as the Distinguished Paul W. Reynolds and Clarice Kingston Reynolds Endowed Chair in Poetry (1997–2007). His books include *Mrs. Belladonna's Supper Club Waltz: New and Selected Prose Poems* (Backwaters Press, 2013), *We Did Not Fear the Father: New and Selected Poems* (Red Hen Press, 2012), *Frankenstein Was a Negro* (Logan House Press, 2002), *Darvil* (St. Andrews Press, 1993), and *The Town Clock Burning* (St. Andrews Press, 1985; Carnegie Mellon Classic Contemporary Series, 1991). The University of Nebraska at Kearney also brought out a number of his chapbooks in limited editions, including *Blues of a Mumbling Train* (2004) and *As the Lilac Burned the Laurel Grew* (1999). Fort's poems have appeared in *The Best American Poetry* (2002 and 2003 editions) and *The Best of the Prose Poem: An International Journal*. He is the founder of the Wendy Fort Foundation Theater of Fine Arts. A MacDowell fellow, Fort is writing his first novel, *The Last Black Hippie in Connecticut*.

Of "One Had Lived in a Room and Loved Nothing," Fort writes: "I am writing 200 villanelles. The book is titled *Sorrow Road*, and its subjects include Stravinsky, Hendrix, Beethoven, Duke Ellington, Van Gogh, the Beatles, Motown, Miles, Coltrane, Pinter, Manson, Charlie McCarthy, Woodstock, Coleridge, Little Black Sambo, Knucklehead Smiff, Bergman, Stephen Hawking, etc. My interest in poetic forms no doubt began with my first reading of A. E. Housman's 'Loveliest of Trees' when I was a lad at our working-class city's public library in New Britain, Connecticut.

"When I told a colleague I was writing 200 villanelles, he said in a soft yet desperate tone: 'No. No. No.' I am grateful to Fred Chappell and Sydney Lea for their enthusiastic support of *Sorrow Road*, which could have been a sonnet sequence (I've written two), a prose-poem sequence (I've written a trilogy), or several sestinas. My last attempt was a variant-triple-sestina full of odd and relentless repetends. Indeed, I wrote a letter to Stephen Hawking at Oxford, not to apply for the job opening to be his assistant, but to ask him if he would assist me in tracing the origin of the *sixes* in the sestina. The matter has yet to be settled.

"I walked into a café ready to sit, read, and write. I observed what I assumed were a mother and daughter ordering their coffee. The daughter seemed distraught. They sat down, the daughter weeping and the mother not recognizing the face of her own daughter, nor the place where they sat and trembled with their simple cups. Over the next few days my poem emerged out of memory and imagination: 'One Had Lived in a Room and Loved Nothing.'"

EMILY FRAGOS has published two books of poetry, *Hostage: New & Selected Poems* (Sheep Meadow Press, 2011) and *Little Savage* (Grove Press, 2004), and has edited five anthologies for the Everyman's Pocket Library. She has received a Guggenheim Fellowship, an award in literature from the American Academy of Arts and Letters, and the Witter Bynner Prize from the Library of Congress. She was born in Mt. Vernon, New York, and she teaches at NYU and Columbia.

Fragos writes: "I discarded a bad poem, but retained one of its phrases: *the sadness of clothes*. This poem flowed from those four words. One can admire the narrator who tries to reason with and accept sorrow; but grief has the final say, as the inconsolable clothes assume their human shapes of despair."

AMY GERSTLER was born in San Diego, California, in 1956. She writes poetry and prose and teaches in the MFA creative writing program at the University of California at Irvine. Her books of poetry include

Scattered at Sea (2015), *Dearest Creature* (2009), *Ghost Girl* (2004), and *Medicine* (2000), all published by Penguin. She was the guest editor of *The Best American Poetry 2010*.

Of "A Drop of Seawater Under the Microscope," Gerstler writes: "The genesis of this poem is very simple, maybe rather childlike. Someone posted a photo on Facebook that I found so mysterious, beautiful, and arresting, of *a drop of seawater under the microscope*. If you are reading this now and get joy from such things, you can Google that phrase and peruse the images that come up. You get pictures of a crazy abundance of microorganisms. These images of what's living and darting about in a drop of ocean water would make awesome wallpaper, or fabric designs. I'd love to have a dress with that print on it. Every time I peer at that busy, active image I am thrilled and sobered by awe and wonder. Some of the life-forms look like streamers, some like conical party hats, some like tiny doodles of eyeballs or breasts, or candies or fireworks or Japanese rice crackers. A drop of seawater as ultimate Rorschach inkblot. So many worlds we can't see, writhing and seething and swimming inside and outside us all. I can never get over it."

DANA GIOIA was born in Los Angeles in 1950. He is the author of five collections of poetry, including *Interrogations at Noon* (Graywolf Press, 2001), which won the American Book Award, and *99 Poems: New & Selected* (Graywolf, 2016). His three critical collections include *Can Poetry Matter?* (Graywolf, 1992). He has written three opera libretti and edited twenty literary anthologies. He served as chairman of the National Endowment for the Arts from 2003 to 2009. He holds the Judge Widney Chair of Poetry and Public Culture at the University of Southern California, where he teaches each fall semester. In 2015 he was appointed the poet laureate of California.

Gioia writes: " 'Meet Me at the Lighthouse' describes a real nightclub on the Hermosa Beach pier in southwest Los Angeles—not far from where I grew up in Hawthorne. The Lighthouse Café never had much ambience, but it survived by showcasing West Coast jazz. The club had a terrific house band, the Lighthouse All-Stars, led by bassist Howard Rumsey. Over the years this smoke-filled, noisy joint featured nearly every major California jazz artist, many of whom recorded there.

"A jazz fan will recognize all of the people named in the poem— Gerry Mulligan, Cannonball Adderley, Hampton Hawes, Stan Getz, Chet Baker, and Art Pepper. I hope Mr. Yeats will forgive my twisting his famous line, but those six musicians do represent some of the 'singing-masters of my soul.' The unnamed 'you' in the poem is my cousin (and closest childhood friend) Philip Dragotto. Since his early death, I've never had the heart to revisit our old haunt. Mr. Bones should require no introduction."

JORIE GRAHAM is the author of eleven collections of poetry, most recently *From the New World: Poems 1976–2014* from Ecco/HarperCollins. She lives in Cambridge, Massachusetts, and teaches at Harvard University. She has received the Pulitzer Prize and a MacArthur Fellowship. She was the guest editor of *The Best American Poetry 1990*.

JULIANA GRAY is the author of *Roleplay* (Dream Horse Press, 2012) and *The Man Under My Skin* (River City Publishing, 2005). Born in Selma, Alabama, in 1972, she now lives in western New York and teaches at Alfred University.

Gray writes: " 'The Lady Responds' came about when I was researching and writing the poems that eventually became my chapbook *Anne Boleyn's Sleeve* (Winged City Chapbook Press, 2013). I was fascinated by the juicy rumor that Anne had had an affair with the poet Thomas Wyatt, and I wanted to give her the chance to respond to Wyatt's overt misogyny in poems like 'Whoso List to Hunt.' The sonnet that resulted, however, didn't fit with the loosely metered, persona-driven Boleyn poems I'd been writing, so I separated it from that project and sent the orphan into the world on its own. I'm grateful to *River Styx* for giving this poem a home, and to Richard Newman for his thoughtful editorial suggestions."

LINDA GREGERSON was born in Elgin, Illinois, in 1950. She is the author of six collections of poetry: *Prodigal: New and Selected Poems: 1976–2014* (Houghton Mifflin Harcourt, 2015), *The Selvage* (Houghton Mifflin Harcourt, 2012), *Magnetic North* (Houghton Mifflin, 2007), *Waterborne* (Houghton Mifflin, 2002), *The Woman Who Died in Her Sleep* (Houghton Mifflin, 1996), and *Fire in the Conservatory* (Dragon Gate, 1982). *Waterborne* won the Kingsley Tufts Poetry Award. A member of the American Academy of Arts and Sciences and a Chancellor of the Academy of American Poets, Gregerson is Distinguished University Professor of English at the University of Michigan, where she directs the Helen Zell Writers' Program.

Of "Font," Gregerson writes: "The article about Baby 59 appeared in *The Guardian* one morning, and I couldn't get it out of my head. So

I trawled the Internet to see if I could learn more about the mother or her child. The accompanying ad was as described. What must we look like to the creatures from other planets who know us only by our algorithms?"

JENNIFER GROTZ was born in Canyon, Texas, in 1971. She is a professor at the University of Rochester and assistant director of the Bread Loaf Writers' Conference. She was named director of the recently established Bread Loaf Translators' Conference. The author of three books of poetry, most recently *Window Left Open* (Graywolf Press, 2016), she has translated works from the French and Polish. Her most recent translations are the novel *Rochester Knockings* by Hubert Haddad (Open Letter, 2015) and *Psalms of All My Days*, poems by Patrice de La Tour du Pin (Carnegie Mellon University Press, 2013). This is her fourth appearance in *The Best American Poetry*.

Of "Self-Portrait on the Street of an Unnamed Foreign City," Grotz writes: "*Ut pictura, poesis*: as with painting, so with poetry, the saying goes, and perhaps this is why from time to time poets, like painters, use the exercise of the self-portrait to practice seeing. If either the poet or the painter is lucky, sight leads to insight. In this unabashedly autobiographical poem, I use a shop window on a busy street in Warsaw, not a mirror, to view myself, and though my poem aims for truthful perception, I think it renders what, I'm convinced more and more, poems are meant to achieve, that is: registering what it feels like to pass through time."

MARK HALLIDAY was born in Ann Arbor, Michigan, in 1949. Since 1996 he has taught in the creative writing program at Ohio University. His sixth book of poems, *Thresherphobe*, appeared in 2013 from the University of Chicago Press.

Of "Doctor Scheef," Halliday writes: "An unreasonable complaint can derive intensity from the speaker's awareness that it is unreasonable. By giving form to such an entangled feeling, a poem can make it less inward-thorny. One good example is 'My Mother's Last Cigarette' by BJ Ward. Another is Dickinson's 'Of course—I prayed—.' And some percentage of the innumerable divorce poems in our world. Sometimes a refusal to forgive is what the spirit needs."

JEFFREY HARRISON was born in Cincinnati, Ohio, in 1957. He has published five books of poetry: *The Singing Underneath* (E. P. Dutton, 1987), selected by James Merrill for the National Poetry Series; *Signs of* opper Beech, 1996); *Feeding the Fire* (Sarabande Books, 2001); *Knowledge* (Four Way Books, 2006); and, most recently, *Into* (Tupelo Press, 2014), the winner of the Dorset Prize. A vol- selected poems, *The Names of Things: New and Selected Poems*, blished in 2006 by the Waywiser Press in the United Kingdom. pient of fellowships from the Guggenheim Foundation and the onal Endowment for the Arts, he lives in eastern Massachusetts.

If "Afterword," Harrison writes: "The maple limb in the poem had ked and fallen under the weight of a wet, heavy snow. It was a large ub, completely detached from the tree and lying on the ground beside rail I walk on periodically in our local woods. I didn't give it a whole ot of thought, but after walking by it for months I'm sure I'd come o think of it as a dead limb. So I was startled one spring day to walk by it and see it in full bloom with small, bright red blossoms (not the buds that become leaves but the tiny red tassel-like flowers that appear earlier). The sight was visually striking in a literal way but also seemed almost instantly emblematic of those moments of magical thinking when loved ones who have died and been separated from us forever suddenly seem to speak or signal to us from the beyond. I was prob- ably thinking of my brother but left him out of this particular poem. Though I often tend to write narratively, this poem was short and more of a lyric from the start, perhaps because it was inspired by, and tries to enact, a sudden moment of recognition."

TERRANCE HAYES was born in Columbia, South Carolina, in 1971. He is the author of *How to Be Drawn* (Penguin, 2015). His other books are *Lighthead* (Penguin, 2010), *Wind in a Box* (Penguin, 2006), *Hip Logic* (Penguin, 2002), and *Muscular Music* (Tia Chucha Press, 1999). He received a 2010 National Book Award and a 2014 MacArthur Fellow- ship. He was the guest editor of *The Best American Poetry 2014*.

Hayes writes: "I hope 'Barberism' lives in the ear. I think of it as a fairly straightforward elegy riding a few rails of sound."

TONY HOAGLAND was born in North Carolina in 1953. His latest book of poems is *Application for Release from the Dream* (2015). Others include *What Narcissism Means to Me* (2003), *Unincorporated Persons in the Late Honda Dynasty* (2010), and *Donkey Gospel* (1998), all from Graywolf Press. His work has received the Mark Twain Award, the James Laugh- lin Prize, the Jackson Poetry Prize, and other recognitions. His second book of prose, *Twenty Poems That Could Save America and Other Essays*, was published by Graywolf in 2014. He teaches creative writing at the University of Houston.

Hoagland writes: "I wrote the poem 'Bible Study' during an especially lucid period a few years ago. I had the feeling that I had made unusual emotional and psychic progress in the preceding year or two, that I had turned a corner in my relations with other people. This had in part to do with friendships formed through my association with an entity called the Great Mother Conference, an annual arts and culture gathering founded forty years ago by Robert Bly. Though who can say about these sea changes of the inner landscape? Some degree of adventure had reentered my life, resulting in the measured optimism of the poem.

"'Bible Study' has what I would call an accretive structure, a counterpoint arrangement of light and brooding tones, alternating ironic and hopeful inflections. Thus the abrupt jump from the wonder of stanza one to the darker tone of stanza two, with its dream image implying that severe damage is fairly inevitable. Similarly, the line that says 'My broken nose is forming an idea of what's for supper' implies a good news/bad news structure to experience: the nose may be broken, but it still works, and there's meatloaf for dinner.

"An accretive or composite poem is not quite like a narrative or discursive poem; it doesn't transport the reader swiftly along in a forward direction; instead, it is like a chord of simultaneously played notes, and the poem's force resides in the combined inferences of harmonic-disharmonic arrangement. And let me say that I myself am mistrustful of aesthetic explanations that sound as conceptual as this one: so much handicapped contemporary poetry uses such nerdy theoretical statements to argue for its own esoteric existence.

"Nonetheless, as I've gotten older, I have found that the narrative modes are not always adequate for representing the layered ambivalences and doubled-creased knowledge that is consciousness past a certain age. Complexity of tone has become, increasingly, the most precious and exciting thing for me in poetry. Tranströmer, Miłosz, Szymborska, Anne Carson, and Fanny Howe—and many others—have become my mentors.

"I'm conscious of the marvelous power of story, and I hope to return to it somehow, but for now it's the music of complex tonal play that I'm drawn to. At the same time, I believe more than ever that emotional depth and its plaintive assertion is the greatest treasure most poems carry, the aspect of poetry that will never grow old or less than neces-

s. That is the impulse in the last stanzas of 'Bible Study.'
ıny ways of delivering the emotional moment of a poem,
think it can be counterfeited or artificed. In that sense,
ʹk is always going to be tied up in self-work, or soul-work, if
to put it like that. As a reader, I feel I can always distinguish
ı the poets who are standing with their feet in the fire, and the
ʋho are phoning it in from uptown."

ɪTHIA HOGUE was born in Rock Island, Illinois, in 1951. She taught
the MFA program at the University of New Orleans before moving
ɔ Pennsylvania, where she directed the Stadler Center for Poetry at
Bucknell University for eight years. While in Pennsylvania, she trained
in conflict resolution with the Mennonites and became a trained media-
tor specializing in diversity issues in education. She has published eight
collections of poetry, three of which—*Revenance* (2014), *Or Consequence*
(2010), and *The Incognito Body* (2006)—were published by Red Hen
Press. Her ninth collection, *In June, the Labyrinth*, will be published by
Red Hen in 2017. Since 2006, Hogue has been an active translator from
contemporary French poetry. She is cotranslator of *Fortino Sámano* (*The
Overflowing of the Poem*) by poet Virginie Lalucq and philosopher Jean-
Luc Nancy, which won the 2013 Harold Morton Landon Translation
Award from the Academy of American Poets. Hogue holds the Maxine
and Jonathan Marshall Chair in modern and contemporary poetry in
the creative writing program at Arizona State University.

Of "The Unwritten Volume," Hogue writes: "This poem is drawn
from a book-length series, *In June, the Labyrinth*, composed of four unti-
tled parts, part elegy and part pilgrimage. During the years in which I
wrote the series, I visited and researched labyrinths, exploring the idea
of the labyrinth as a figure for the poem (and for a life). That central
trope emerges in 'The Unwritten Volume,' a poem that includes details
from one of my first trips to Chartres Cathedral, as I was about to learn
that a dear friend I knew to be ailing had died. The trip to Chartres
triggered a kind of vague, initiatory idea: something has begun but you
have no idea for some time where it's going. Even, maybe, nowhere.
You just have to find out, that much you know. Along with the literary
allusions in 'The Unwritten Volume,' there emerge the odd or disso-
nant narrative elements, like the little boy scattering the rose petals, a
remembered dinner in a termite-infested cottage, and the organist (who
had been playing for a wedding) sticking around to practice his Bach.
As the original loss of my friend deepened with other losses, the central

character became a fictional composite, 'Elle,' whose story began to come to me quite separate from any life I knew my friend to have lived, except for the fact that she never had time to finish her book. Perhaps it's obvious that my book isn't hers, but it contains a palimpsest of the quest she undertook and didn't live to finish."

GARRETT HONGO was born in Volcano, Hawai'i, and grew up on the North Shore of O'ahu and in Los Angeles. He was educated at Pomona College, the University of Michigan, and the University of California at Irvine, where he received an MFA. His latest book of poetry, *Coral Road*, was published by Alfred A. Knopf in 2011. He has also published two books of poetry, three anthologies, and *Volcano: A Memoir of Hawai'i* (Knopf/Vintage, 1995). He has received a Guggenheim Fellowship, two NEA grants, a Fulbright Fellowship, and the Lamont Poetry Prize from the Academy of American Poets. He has taught at Houston, UC Irvine, Vanderbilt, and the Universitá degli Studi di Firenze. A Distinguished Professor of Arts and Sciences at the University of Oregon, he is at work on a book of nonfiction entitled *The Perfect Sound: Confessions of an Audiophile*.

Of "I Got Heaven," Hongo writes: "The poem came about in an unusual way. In January 2014 or so, the poet and HarperCollins editor Daniel Halpern asked me to contribute my original manuscript pages of a poem for an auction he was planning in support of the National Poetry Series—a very worthy cause. I thought I'd contribute the draft pages of a poem that had appeared in his magazine *Antaeus* back in the 1980s, but I couldn't locate them. Instead, I found a file marked '79 Drafts in ballpoint on the bent and fraying tab. It contained stray lines, on yellow sheets, that must have been my first attempt to write about the Obon festival in Gardena, California, where I went to high school. Gardena is a suburb of Los Angeles where, eventually, about sixteen thousand Japanese Americans came to live when they were released from internment camps after World War II—the highest concentration of Japanese Americans outside of Honolulu. It's also right next to Compton, where my African American schoolmates got bused in to attend Gardena High. A flatland where once had been fields of strawberries and flowers, the area is dotted with touches of Japanese culture everywhere—full-size front yard pines trimmed and twisted like bonsai, shops selling sushi and Japanese pastries, and traditional architectural structures like the Nishi Hongwanji Buddhist Temple on 166th Street. In midsummer, the church sponsors a 'festival for the dead.' People of all ethnicities from all over the community gather, wearing color-ful happi coats, brocaded kimono with flowing sleeves, and summer evening robes of thin cotton, to dance in a joyous circle up and down the roped-off street next to the temple. The music has a heavy drum beat. The theology is that it's to earn better karma for souls of the dead trapped in limbo, unable to reach nirvana. Your dancing frees them. I'd always wanted to write about that event, full of such splendor, and here, in draft pages, were lines from the first time I'd tried. They were scribbled down when I'd been a graduate student at UC Irvine, study-ing under the great poet Charles Wright. But they'd gone nowhere. I couldn't find my way to a poem then. In times since, I've written other poems about Obon festivals in Kahuku, Waimea, and Hale'iwa, all in Hawai'i, where I lived as a child, but never from a festival in Gardena. But seeing these stray, effortful lines again, I knew immediately what to do. So I composed a new piece, resetting some of the lines and most of the images from this old draft. The poem came out easily. I sent the old manuscript pages, the one page of the new draft, and a typescript copy of the finished poem to Dan, and I think he incorporated them in his auction. 'I Got Heaven' is this poem."

ERIN HOOVER was born in 1979 in Harrisburg, Pennsylvania, and cur-rently lives in Tallahassee, Florida, where she is a doctoral candidate at Florida State University. She has served as editor of *The Southeast Review*, a volunteer for VIDA: Women in Literary Arts, and cofounder of Late Night Library, a literary arts nonprofit organization. For about a decade she lived in New York City and worked as a communications director.

Of "Girls," Hoover writes: "Long before I thought I had any right to be a feminist poet and academic, I considered myself a feminist per-son—yet it was never clear to me how to be one on a daily basis. I knew what I believed, but not how to enact my beliefs with any decisiveness as a person in the world. When Lena Dunham and HBO launched *Girls*, I thought, yes, that's what this show is about. The three waves of feminism exist on a continuum, and so do all the women who have ever stood at the back of a club waiting to get chosen by the band, in an environment which is fraught not only with the economies of sex and ambition, but also just plain wanting validation in whatever form it comes. The critical reaction to *Girls* reminded me of all the ways that women continue to have our actions defined for us by a culture that is extremely hostile if we won't play the game. So when I say, 'turn up the lights,' I mean let's acknowledge that all of this is complicated, and know that we can hold strong political beliefs and still desire attention and affection from others, sometimes under terms we don't get to set. Both things are true."

Born in Ohio in 1929, RICHARD HOWARD was educated in an intensely progressive institution called the Park School of Cleveland, thereafter graduating from Columbia College and receiving an MA from Columbia University, followed in 1953 by a fellowship at the Sorbonne. Remaining in Paris for several years, he later worked for three years as a lexicographer in Cleveland and New York, since then writing fifteen books of poems, several volumes of criticism, and some two hundred works of translation from French, including works by Gide, Roland Barthes, Stendhal, Baudelaire, and de Gaulle. He has received a National Book Award for his translation of *Les Fleurs du mal* and a Pulitzer Prize for *Untitled Subjects*, a collection of poetry. In 2014 his latest book of poems, *A Progressive Education*, was published by Turtle Point Press. For the last seventeen years he has taught literature to aspiring young poets in the School of the Arts, Writing Division, at Columbia. He was the guest editor of *The Best American Poetry 1995*.

T. R. HUMMER was born in Macon, Mississippi, in 1950, "and escaped from there with my soul hidden away in a Prince Albert can and stuffed in a tenor sax case in 1976." His twelfth book of poems, *Eon*—which is the third in a cluster of three books, ten years in the making—will be published by Louisiana State University Press in 2018. He teaches distantly for Arizona State University.

Hummer writes: " 'Minutiae' was born by accident, out of the ruin of a misguided attempt to write a poem about the songwriter Hank Williams. There are lines in his great song 'I'm So Lonesome I Could Cry' that have long interested me as a poet: 'Did you ever see a robin weep / When leaves begin to die?' is surely (I have often thought) one of the most wretched couplets ever penned. No, I say, I never did see a robin weep. How would you know a robin was weeping? Would a great tear roll down his feathery cheek out there in the woods where the leaves of course are dying? But then Williams pulls it out: 'That means he's lost the will to live / I'm so lonesome I could cry.' At that point we see perfectly how the 'pathetic fallacy' operates, how the personification is a perfect projection of the singer's emotional disaster. The devil is in the minutiae, but the soul is revealed in the stark gesture: *he's* lost the will to live, but *I* am so lonesome I could cry. Cue the pedal steel guitar. The poem about Williams was stillborn, but the desire remained. That swerve was the thing I wanted to replicate, the steel guitar's rending glissando, and the resulting wreckage."

Ishion Hutchinson was born in Port Antonio, Jamaica. His poetry collections are *Far District: Poems* (Peepal Tree Press, 2010) and *House of Lords and Commons: Poems* (Farrar, Straus and Giroux, 2016). He is the Meringoff Sesquicentennial Fellow assistant professor of English at Cornell University and a contributing editor to the literary journal *Tongue: A Journal of Writing & Art.*

Hutchinson writes: "I wrote, or rather rewrote, the first draft of what became 'Morning Tableau' one morning last summer in Krems, Austria. The poem's previous incarnation had the image of the beloved swaying in the hammock and the little lyric, 'my God, my heaven, my all,' which came from reading a letter of Van Gogh's in which he quotes a hymn (to Tio, I think) from *Uncle Tom's Cabin*, a book he loved. The morning I woke to rain—rain on the Danube, which I could see from my window over the tops of apartments—and maybe this will sound melodramatic, but the rain didn't seem like rain at home, no tropical haze, if I may, but it stuck with me and the atmosphere, the romance of the Austrian rain, ashen to my eyes (light tropical rain being clear silver), started to work its way into the draft. I am sure it was the rain that led me to rewrite the poem, but it was the town as a whole. One of the streets near the hotel is lined with linden, there is even a hotel there called Unter den Linden, which, I supposed, is to be reminiscent of the boulevard in Berlin, and of course it is nowhere as grand; this is a provincial town, its association is rural medieval, not of the operatic architecture of a wet metropolis, just the subtle resonance you find of a village in the rain anywhere. A scream is buried under every quiet, something disfigured by history, and I think the poem eventually rejects the quiet it opens with, rejects even an attitude that says love is paradisal, to end on an inflection of morning as mourning, depending on your accent. That disfiguring history in the poem is, of course, the Holocaust and World War II, which I think is filtered through some of the books I was reading then, particularly those of Thomas Bernhard. I didn't want to be emphatic about that—essentially I see the poem as a love poem, an aubade—hence why the most direct line concerning that history is borrowed and bracketed with quotation marks."

MAJOR JACKSON is the author of four collections of poetry, most recently *Roll Deep* (W. W. Norton, 2015). A recipient of a Guggenheim Fellowship, he is the Richard A. Dennis Professor at the University of Vermont and a member of the core faculty at the Bennington Writing Seminars. He is poetry editor of the *Harvard Review*.

Jackson writes: " 'Aubade' takes off from Richard Wilbur's terrific poem 'A Late Aubade,' whose rhetorical structure sponsors my own poem. Prior to 2012, I thought the tradition of poetry about lovers separating in the morning a quaint layover from that bygone era of courtly love poetry whose passionate expressions of longing seemed excessively sentimental and out of step with our times. Until forced to conduct and manage a relationship over 1,300 miles for nearly half a decade in which the anxiety of separation from my wife and of having to say 'good-bye' was real in every instance, did I change my attitude and begin to take delight in such poetry whose themes of carpe diem and living a full life inclusive of spiritual and corporeal love felt essential and timeless, recognizing, too, that such dramatic performances of seduction are not only a necessity of the form, but a joy when adapted to refract the particular texture of loving in our fast-paced age of travel and digital connectedness. Like the sonnet, the aubade understands itself as participating in a conversation about love *and* as a performance rather than a confession whose audience is more than the beloved addressed in the poem, but the countless readers who will encounter it."

Born in Detroit in 1948, LAWRENCE JOSEPH is a graduate of the University of Michigan, where he received a major Hopwood Award for poetry; the University of Cambridge, where he received an MA in English Literature; and the University of Michigan Law School. His most recent books of poetry are *Into It* and *Codes, Precepts, Biases, and Taboos: Poems 1973–1993* (which includes his first three books, *Shouting at No One, Curriculum Vitae,* and *Before Our Eyes*), published in 2005 by Farrar, Straus and Giroux. His book of poems *So Where Are We?* is forthcoming from FSG in 2017. He is also the author of two books of prose, *Lawyerland* (FSG, 1997) and *The Game Changed: Essays and Other Prose,* published in the University of Michigan Press's Poets on Poetry Series in 2011. He has received the Agnes Lynch Starrett Prize for *Shouting at No One* and fellowships from the National Endowment for the Arts and the Guggenheim Foundation. As Tinnelly Professor of Law at St. John's University School of Law, he teaches courses on labor, employment, and tort and compensation law, legal theory, and law and interpretation. He has also taught creative writing at Princeton. Married to the painter Nancy Van Goethem, he lives in lower Manhattan.

Joseph writes: " 'Visions of Labor' draws on a number of sources. I was born and raised in Detroit and, except for two fellowship years in Cambridge, England, I lived in Detroit or in nearby Ann Arbor until my early thirties when my wife and I moved to New York City. My parents, children of Lebanese and Syrian immigrants, were born in Detroit and lived their entire lives there. When my father's and uncle's grocery-liquor store in Detroit could no longer support two families, my father worked for the A&P as a meat cutter while working at the store three nights a week. We were, in socioeconomic terms, lower-middle, working class. My father retired a proud and grateful union member, as did uncles of mine.

"As a Catholic, on the Catholic Left, I've closely read the papal social encyclicals on labor and capital, and have been involved with the Catholic Worker Movement; politically, I've always been positioned to the left of what was the social democracy of Walter Reuther's UAW. For over a year, I worked on assembly lines in Chrysler and General Motors factories, and in press-machine shops, in Detroit and Pontiac, Michigan. During my forty years as a lawyer and law professor, I've practiced, taught, written, and lectured on labor and employment law, especially workers compensation. My poetry, essays, and prose works have from the start included issues of labor and capital, class and race.

"In its broadest sense, 'Visions of Labor' presents a language of labor that purposely reflects a moral vision. Among its formal-structural-rhetorical influences are Ezra Pound's 'Canto XVI'; Louis Zukofsky's 'A'-8; Allen Ginsberg's 'Wichita Vortex Sutra'; Adrienne Rich's *An Atlas of the Difficult World*; and Robert Hayden's '[American Journal].' "

JULIE KANE was born in Boston, Massachusetts, in 1952. Despite her Boston Irish roots, she has lived in Louisiana for four decades now and served as the Louisiana poet laureate from 2011 to 2013. She is a professor of English at Northwestern State University in Natchitoches. Her poetry books are *Paper Bullets* (White Violet Press, 2014), a collection of light verse; *Jazz Funeral* (Story Line Press, 2009), the winner of the 2009 Donald Justice Poetry Prize (David Mason, judge); *Rhythm & Booze* (University of Illinois Press, 2003), Maxine Kumin's selection for the 2002 National Poetry Series; and *Body and Soul* (Pirogue Publishing, 1987).

Of "As If," Kane writes: "Strangely, the image that gave rise to the

poem did not wind up in the poem. Many years ago
play that ended with a dead body lying on the stage. W
for curtain calls, the body jumped up and took his b
of the cast. That moment of surprise and childlike deli
dead man spring back to life made a strong impression
later when a long-dead relationship was resuscitated, it l
to mind—though a real corpse took the place of the st
resulting poem. But I guess the metaphorical applaus
might be a nod to the poem's origins. And of course, t
to be a sonnet because that's the form most associated v
I hope that the language sounds conversational despit
meter."

SUJI KWOCK KIM's parents and grandparents were all
now North Korea, where her grandfather, uncle, aunt,
live. She is the author of *Notes from the Divided Country*
Walt Whitman Award from the Academy of America
Private Property, a multimedia play performed at the
tival Fringe; and *Disorient*, which is forthcoming. She
of fellowships from the National Endowment for the
IIE, the Association for Asian Studies, the Blakemore
Asian Studies, the Korea Foundation, the Japan Found
institutions. Her work has been performed by the Toky
Chorus and recorded for National Public Radio and
Broadcasting Corporation. An earlier version of "Returi
won the George Bogin Memorial Award from the P
America in 2012.

Kim writes: " 'Return of the Native' is part of a l
exploring the questions of remembering and forgetting,
ing, interiority and exteriority, in the context of North K
veillance and snitching mean loyalty to the regime and
be 'performed,' while an estimated 150,000–200,000 pc
work in the labor camps, which are clearly visible in
although the regime denies that they exist. This is a cou
Il-Sung is 'Eternal President,' the only corpse in the wor
utive office, although he's been dead for more than twer

"I've never met my grandfather, and my father last sa
was ten years old. When I was doing research in a smal
west of London called New Malden—it has the larges
North Korean refugees outside Asia, surprisingly, more

ited States—I met a man about the same age as my grandfather, who
ne from a village not far from his. (In the dedication, his name and
metown have been altered, to protect his family.) Their lives have
eral other parallels, with one exception, of course: he escaped, and
grandfather did not.

"I'm deeply grateful to Mr. K., who generously took the time to help
understand a little of what he lived through, and by extension, a
le of what my grandfather must have lived through, the grandfather
never know."

RETTA COLLINS KLOBAH was born in the San Joaquin Valley of Cali-
nia in 1961. She has lived in San Juan, Puerto Rico, for two decades,
teaches Caribbean literature, creative writing, and courses related
the medical humanities at the University of Puerto Rico. She had
viously lived in Jamaica, England, and Canada. She earned an MFA
oetry writing from the Writers' Workshop at the University of Iowa,
ere she also completed a doctoral degree in English. Her poetry col-
tion *The Twelve Foot Neon Woman* (Peepal Tree Press, 2011) received
2012 OCM Bocas Prize in Caribbean Literature in the category of
try (Trinidad and Tobago). The Literary Arts section of the Puerto
an newspaper *El Nuevo Día* named it one of the top ten books of
year (2012) by a Puerto Rican author. She has recently been a guest
t at the Bim Lit Fest in Barbados, the Bocas Lit Fest in Trinidad and
bago, the book fair in St. Martin, and the Calabash Literary Festival
amaica.

Klobah writes: "The poem 'Tissue Gallery' describes, with exactitude,
pe, a small collection of 'human tissue' specimens that I was invited
iew at a medical school in Puerto Rico, where I live. Given that var-
s medical museums do exhibit—for educational purposes—medical
ities, preserved fetuses in jars, specimens that demonstrate pathology
nomaly, wax models, antique, seemingly macabre medical instru-
ts or flayed cadavers, the speaker's physician-friend's proposal for
stically exhibiting the specimens is not odd. At the Mütter Museum
he College of Physicians of Philadelphia, for instance, one may ogle
liver of the conjoined twins Chang and Eng, as well as a number of
erved fetuses. These medical museums are seen as respectable, com-
d to the circus sideshows, freak shows, penny arcades, and curiosity
nets where 'pickled punks' have been displayed.

A few people at a time were escorted into the lab room where the
ection had been set out. As the poem indicates, I didn't previously

realize that I would be seeing this kind of 'human tissue.' I was the last person to leave the room. I thought of the women who had carried these stillborns. I thought of our historical context here in the Caribbean. Drawing upon a Caribbean cosmology, the poem acknowledges these little ones who are both here and not here, but still have the power to move us. For me, although it raises issues of ethics, language, and race, it is not a poem to be read in an overly determined way in the context of U.S. abortion debates about pro-choice/pro-life. It does not advocate for limiting a woman's freedom of choice, which, as a woman and mother, I believe in. It is a praise song, a *velorio*; it is a whisper for sisterhood. The public exhibition has not taken place."

JOHN KOETHE was born in San Diego in 1945. He received an AB from Princeton in 1967 and a PhD in philosophy from Harvard in 1973. He is Distinguished Professor of Philosophy Emeritus at the University of Wisconsin–Milwaukee. He has published ten books of poetry and has been awarded the Frank O'Hara, Kingsley Tufts, and Lenore Marshall awards. His most recent poetry books are *The Swimmer* (Farrar, Straus and Giroux, 2016) and *ROTC Kills* (HarperCollins, 2012). He has written books on Wittgenstein and on philosophical skepticism as well as a collection of literary essays. He lives in Milwaukee.

Of "The Swimmer," Koethe writes: "In the 1970s and '80s my ex-wife and I used to spend a week each summer on a lake in Michigan's Upper Peninsula, and on one of those visits in 1982 I read a lot of John Cheever's short stories and subsequently wrote a poem, 'In the Park,' that appeared in my book *The Late Wisconsin Spring* (Princeton University Press, 1984), and which I thought had a kind of Cheeveresque feel to it. A few years ago I was reading a book about six alcoholic writers, of whom Cheever was one. It discussed his famous story 'The Swimmer,' that I was sure I'd read back in 1982, though its description of the story didn't ring a bell. I looked at the story and realized I'd never read it in the first place, or if I had, I'd completely forgotten it. I started writing a memory poem centered on the story and on that distant summer, using the stanza form and something like the tone of 'In the Park,' resulting in the poem here, which I titled after Cheever's story."

YUSEF KOMUNYAKAA's books of poetry include *Taboo*, *Dien Cai Dau*, *Neon Vernacular* (for which he received the Pulitzer Prize), *The Chameleon Couch*, *The Emperor of Water Clocks*, and *Testimony: A Tribute to*

Charlie Parker. He has received the William Faulkner Prize (Université de Rennes, France), the Kingsley Tufts Poetry Award, the Ruth Lilly Poetry Prize, and the 2011 Wallace Stevens Award. His plays, performance art, and libretti have been performed internationally. They include *Slipknot*, *Wakonda's Dream*, *Nine Bridges Back*, *Saturnalia*, *Testimony*, *The Mercy Suite*, and *Gilgamesh: A Verse Play* (with Chad Garcia). He teaches at New York University. He was the guest editor of *The Best American Poetry 2003*.

Of "The Fool," Komunyakaa writes: "I have always thought of the fool in classical literature and folklore as the wise man or proxy king, and sometimes he's the freest of the lot. He is a master of satire and his linguistic daring is usually edgy, succinct, and political. Likewise, when considering more modern versions of the fool, I particularly think of Lenny Bruce, Jackie 'Moms' Mabley, and Richard Pryor. We admire the fool's skill and finesse in critiquing fractions of absolute power. Perhaps that is why in hard times we embrace our comedy clubs, replaying vaudevillian skits—the theater of ridicule. Ironically such a subversive symbol of power survives because he or she is an appendage, a go-between, or a mouthpiece. In a classical sense, the fool is the king's alter ego. The lone figure goes up against an institution. Sometimes the fool is free to say what the king cannot say to himself. He is the king for a moment. But with the snap of a finger the axe could fall. The king and the fool are fully aware, and this becomes a contest of perverted fun."

KEETJE KUIPERS was born in Pullman, Washington, in 1980. She has been the Margery Davis Boyden Wilderness Writing Resident, a Stegner Fellow at Stanford, and the Emerging Writer Lecturer at Gettysburg College. Her first book of poems, *Beautiful in the Mouth*, won the 2009 A. Poulin, Jr. Poetry Prize and was published by BOA Editions, Ltd. Her second collection, *The Keys to the Jail*, was published by BOA in 2014. She is an associate professor at Auburn University, where she is editor of *Southern Humanities Review*.

Of "We drive home from the lake, sand in our shoes," Kuipers writes: "This poem began with the image of the sheriff lighting the cigarette—something I saw on a drive through rural Alabama not long after moving there nearly three years ago. That image stuck with me, but I didn't know what it meant yet or how I would use it. Along the way I collected additional images from my new life in the South, along with a number of resonant place-names, including the town of Notasulga, which is not far from where we live. Finally, I wrote this poem last year, and just a few months later married my longtime partner, a moment fourteen years (and plenty of heartache) in the making."

DEBORAH LANDAU is the author of *The Uses of the Body* (2015) and *The Last Usable Hour* (2011), both Lannan Literary Selections from Copper Canyon Press, and *Orchidelirium* (2004), which was selected by Naomi Shihab Nye for the Robert Dana-Anhinga Prize for Poetry. Her work has been featured on NPR's *All Things Considered*. She directs the creative writing program at New York University, where she also teaches.

Landau writes: " 'Solitaire' is an extract from my third book, *The Uses of the Body*, which considers the pleasures and complexities of living in a female body, and of marriage and domestic life. The book is comprised of linked lyric sequences—a form I've come to love because it allows perspective on the same subject from many angles for a cumulative, prismatic effect. 'Solitaire' rides on the myriad anxieties of living in a body as time passes. Like much of my writing it is driven by music—I let the sounds carry it along. 'I don't have a pill for that' is a favorite saying of a favorite doctor of mine."

LI-YOUNG LEE was born in Jakarta, Indonesia, in 1957. He is the author of the poetry collections *Rose*, *The City in Which I Love You*, *Book of My Nights* (all from BOA Editions, Ltd., in 1993, 1990, and 2001), and *Behind My Eyes* (W. W. Norton, 2009), as well as the book-length prose poem *The Winged Seed* (Simon & Schuster, 1995). He has a full-length collection forthcoming from W. W. Norton. He lives in Chicago with his wife.

PHILIP LEVINE (1928–2015) was born into a family of Russian-Jewish immigrants and worked in Detroit auto factories from the age of fourteen. Described by Edward Hirsch as "a large, ironic Whitman of the industrial heartland," Levine was the celebrated author of more than twenty poetry collections and a legendary teacher who influenced countless young poets from California State University, Fresno, on the West Coast to NYU and Columbia on the East. In 2011 he was appointed Poet Laureate of the United States. In *The Bread of Time: Toward an Autobiography*, he wrote about his experiences as a factory worker and about such of his mentors as Berryman and Yvor Winters. About Berryman he commented, "He was a guy who didn't want you writing like him. He considered himself, and rightly so, as a rather eccentric poet, and he urged me away from that kind of eccentricity."

Levine told his *Paris Review* interviewer that he used to memorize poems "when I worked in factories and recited them to myself. The noise was so stupendous. Some people singing, some people talking to themselves, a lot of communication going on with nothing, no one to hear." Levine's final two books are scheduled for publication in November 2016 by Alfred A. Knopf: *The Last Shift*, a collection of poems, and *My Lost Poets*, a prose book.

LARRY LEVIS (1946–1996) was born in Fresno, California. He grew up as a ranch boy in the small town of Selma, the "raisin capital of the universe." Working as a janitor in a steel mill, he started writing poetry at California State University, Fresno, where he studied with Philip Levine, who became a lifelong friend. "That an unathletic, acne-ridden virgin who owned the slowest car in town should at age sixteen decide to become a poet struck [Levis] as both outrageous and perfectly right," Levine writes. Levis went on to receive his BA from Syracuse University and his PhD from the University of Iowa. He published five collections of poetry during his lifetime. Three volumes have appeared posthumously: *Elegy* (Pitt Poetry Series, 1997), edited by Philip Levine, *The Selected Levis* (Pitt Poetry Series, 2000), and *The Darkening Trapeze: Last Poems* (Graywolf Press, 2016), both edited by David St. John. "When I am weary of the mediocrity or smallness of so much that passes for poetry, I go to Larry's work and revive my belief in the value of the art we shared," Levine wrote.

ROBIN COSTE LEWIS is the author of *Voyage of the Sable Venus* (Alfred A. Knopf, 2015), which won the 2015 National Book Award in poetry. She is a Provost's Fellow in poetry and visual studies at the University of Southern California. She is also a Cave Canem fellow and a fellow of the Los Angeles Institute for the Humanities. She received her MFA in poetry from NYU, and an MTS in Sanskrit and comparative religious literature from Harvard Divinity School. She has taught at Wheaton College, Hunter College, Hampshire College, and the NYU Low-Residency MFA program in Paris. She was born in Compton, California; her family is from New Orleans.

Lewis writes: "At its most central motivation, 'On the Road to Sri Bhuvaneshwari' is an homage to the Goddess Parvati. I wanted to write something that pleased Her—a poem as an offering, something that could say thank you for destroying my ridiculous life. I appreciate, very much, certain ideologies that ask us to understand our individual lives as private expressions of the divine. Within that frame, everyone, including oneself, is a manifestation of the divine—in this case, the Goddess. The problem with this ideal, of course, is that life is a helluvalot harder, sicker, darker than any ideology. It has to be lived, practiced—not merely discussed: So your partner—that ass!—is really the Goddess hiding behind a mask (this mask called 'the body'). And here's the kick—She's hiding just for you. I also wrote this poem because I wanted to explore what happens when the most precious thing dies, literally. It wasn't merely the dissolving of a relationship that held my attention; it was more serious than that: Love Herself was walking away. Because I was of a certain age with very few pearls left to clutch—I was trying to understand that kind of devastation from a different perspective. I'm suspicious about heteronormativity, how insidious it is. Even our breakups are constructed, scripted. I was looking for a richer way to represent falling out of love.

"But all that came after years and years of silence. On the day that I finally sat down to write this poem, I didn't know what I was doing. Each line felt like a quick sketch. I just started writing, or listening. I had been thinking a lot about India, where I had lived on and off for a while. It's hard to think about India without thinking about the East India Company and the West India Company—colonialism always present in everything I do, like the ancient world. But still this poem felt accidental. I was smarting. One day it pretty much came out just as it is, beginning to end. That rarely happens. I believe in the Great Church of Revision, so this poem falling out fully fashioned shocked me. And when it turned in on itself, at the end, it was its gift for me. In writing it, I learned who the new self was to become. I love that great Hindu/Buddhist slogan: 'There are no others.' I was feeling that deeply. There was no one to blame. Certainly no one to praise. So much death, and not all of it obvious. I was thinking about the ways in which we take our leave—from homes, from nations, from our bodies, from each other. And most of all I wanted to say to the Goddess: Life sucks, but I understand. Perhaps this poem was proof of my surrender."

THOMAS LUX was born in 1946 in Massachusetts. His most recent book of poetry is *To the Left of Time* (Houghton Mifflin Harcourt, 2016). In 2017, Farrar, Straus and Giroux will publish *I Am Flying into Myself: Selected Poems of Bill Knott*, which Lux edited and for which he wrote the introduction. He is Bourne Professor of Poetry at the Georgia Institute of Technology. He lives in Atlanta.

Of "Ode While Awaiting Execution," Lux writes: "The poem was composed over a period of several months in 2014. The poem uses one of my favorite poetic tools: metaphor. I wish I could speak more about the process of writing a poem, but except for saying that it happens gradually over many drafts, I can't."

PAUL MARIANI was born in New York City on February 29, 1940. He holds a chair as Boston College's University Professor of English, where he has taught since 2000. Prior to that he was Distinguished University Professor at the University of Massachusetts, where he taught from 1968 until 2000. His first teaching assignments were at Colgate University, the semester we lost Jack Kennedy, and three colleges in the New York City area: Hunter, Lehman, and the John Jay College of Criminal Justice, where Frank Serpico was one of his students. Mariani is the author of eighteen books, including seven volumes of poetry: *Timing Devices* (Pennyroyal Press and Godine; 1977, 1979), *Crossing Cocytus* (Grove Press, 1982), *Prime Mover* (Grove Press, 1985), *Salvage Operations: New and Selected Poems* (W. W. Norton, 1990), *The Great Wheel* (Norton, 1996), *Deaths & Transfigurations* (Paraclete Press, 2005), and *Epitaphs for the Journey: New, Selected, and Revised Poems* (Cascade Books, 2012). In addition he has published *A Commentary on the Complete Poems of Gerard Manley Hopkins* (Cornell University Press, 1970), *William Carlos Williams: The Poet and His Critics* (American Library Association, 1974), *A Usable Past: Essays on Modern & Contemporary Poetry* (University of Massachusetts Press, 1984), *God and the Imagination: Poetry, Poets, and the Ineffable* (University of Georgia Press, 2002), *Thirty Days: On Retreat with the Exercises of St. Ignatius* (Viking/Penguin, 2002), and six biographies of poets: *William Carlos Williams: A New World Naked* (McGraw Hill and Norton, 1981 and 1990); *Dream Song: The Life of John Berryman* (William Morrow, 1990); *Lost Puritan: A Life of Robert Lowell* (Norton, 1994); *The Broken Tower: A Life of Hart Crane* (Norton, 1999), which was the basis for James Franco's feature-length film *The Broken Tower*; *Gerard Manley Hopkins: A Life* (Viking/Penguin, 2008); and *The Whole Harmonium: The Life of Wallace Stevens* (Simon & Schuster, 2016).

Of "Psalm for the Lost," Mariani writes: "I don't remember exactly what was troubling me when I wrote this poem, and in truth I don't really want to go back there again. But what the poem tells me is that I had finally come to the realization in the very marrow of my soul that everything I had worked for or thought I had worked for would soon come to an end, and that I had no control over what my gift to others—if anything—will be. Fr. Hopkins knew this, as did John Berryman. But then so, too, did others I have followed down the years: Hardy, Yeats, Williams, Stevens, Lowell, Hart Crane, Flannery O'Connor, Philip Levine. My wife and I read a psalm each morning over coffee as a kind of spiritual exercise, and so something of the ancient cry you find there finds itself here as well. But then there's Thomas Aquinas, the great theologian, who realized at the end that everything he had built was just so much straw in comparison to what he glimpsed at the altar one morning. Then, too, there's Caravaggio's sobering portrait of Peter at the moment of his denial of his master, caught in the unforgiving light of that brazier, and the troubling question of what after all really matters if you can deny everything you've built your life on. Which brings me to the Zen-like final image of my three sons building the most elaborate sand castles for our five grandchildren each summer on First Encounter Beach—turrets, art deco, Gaudi-like structures, which the incoming tide washes away within hours. If anything I have built is going to remain, it will have to be in hands other than my own, building up, as the wind wills, once again out of the dust."

DEBRA MARQUART is a professor of English in the MFA Program in creative writing and environment at Iowa State University. She is the senior editor of *Flyway: Journal of Writing and Environment* and an affiliated faculty member with the Stonecoast low-residency MFA program at the University of Southern Maine. She is the author of three poetry collections—*Small Buried Things* (New Rivers Press, 2015), *Everything's a Verb* (New Rivers, 1995), and *From Sweetness* (Pearl Editions, 2001)—and a short story collection, *The Hunger Bone: Rock & Roll Stories* (New Rivers, 2001). *The Horizontal World: Growing up Wild in the Middle of Nowhere* (Counterpoint Press, 2007), her memoir, received the "Elle Lettres" award from *Elle* magazine and the 2007 PEN USA Creative Nonfiction Award. She won the 2013 Wachtmeister Award from the Virginia Center for the Creative Arts, the Normal Poetry Prize from *The Normal School*, and the 2014 Paumanok Poetry Award from Farmingdale State College.

Marquart writes: " 'Lament' is the last section of the long title poem of my latest collection, *Small Buried Things*. The poem documents the destructive effects of the oil exploration that has overrun my home state of North Dakota since the discovery of two shale formations underlying the state that have an estimated 7 to 11 billion barrels of oil—made recoverable now through the technology of fracking. The sections of the poem register my own concerns, plus the worries that I heard from people within the region as I traveled the state in 2013 and 2015 teaching writing workshops for the North Dakota Humanities Council in small towns and communities impacted by the oil boom.

"According to *The New York Times*, in the period between 2006 and 2014, 'more than 18.4 million gallons of oils and chemicals spilled, leaked or misted into the air, soil and waters of North Dakota. . . . In addition, the oil industry reported spilling 5.2 million gallons of nontoxic substances, mostly fresh water, which can alter the environment and carry contaminants.' These spills occurred largely in rural parts of the state without access to municipal water supplies where populations are dependent on well water drawn from groundwater sources made vulnerable by surface spills.

"The first four sections of the poem, 'Small Buried Things,' address the degradation to the environment, the impacts on soil, water safety, and human health, as well as the sharp rise in violent crime, industrial accidents, and highway fatalities. The poem also addresses the concerning presence of actively commissioned ICBMs that remain buried in the region where fracking is occurring, in addition to concerns about the rise in seismic activity through the midwestern states because of reinjection wells, another byproduct technology connected to the practice of fracking. 'Lament' is the last section of the poem, a kind of keening in the face of what has proven to be the unstoppable destructive force of the oil extraction industry."

CATE MARVIN was born in Washington, DC, in 1969. She attended Marlboro College in Vermont for her BA. She received two MFAs in creative writing, one from the University of Houston in poetry, the other from the Iowa Writers' Workshop in fiction, as well as a PhD in English from the University of Cincinnati. She has published three books of poems: *World's Tallest Disaster* (Sarabande Books, 2001), *Fragment of the Head of a Queen* (Sarabande, 2007), and *Oracle* (W. W. Norton, 2015). She has received the Kate Tufts Discovery Award, a Whiting Writers' Award, and a Guggenheim Fellowship. She lives in Maplewood, New Jersey, with her daughter, and is a professor of English and creative writing at the College of Staten Island, City University of New York.

Marvin writes: "Thanks to the generosity of my then-Dean at the College of Staten Island, Francisco Soto (himself a scholar of Octavio

Paz), I was granted a three-week academic tour of China during the summer of 2007, an experience upon which the poem 'High School in Schuzou' was based. I'd long been loath to consider my high school experience as poetic material. However, while visiting a particular school in Schuzou, I went to a restroom (a 'girls' room') and experienced a flashback: in short, I felt confined, and was intensely reminded that we *all* originate from a point of certain disadvantage as children placed in institutional environments. My most recent book, *Oracle*, contains several 'high school' poems that explore this experience."

MORGAN PARKER was born in 1987 in Redlands, California, and currently lives in Brooklyn, New York. She is the author of *Other People's Comfort Keeps Me Up at Night* (Switchback Books, 2015), selected by Eileen Myles for the 2013 Gatewood Prize. Her second collection, *There Are More Beautiful Things Than Beyoncé*, is forthcoming from Tin House Books in February 2017. A Cave Canem graduate fellow, she works as an editor for Amazon Publishing's imprint Little A, and moonlights as poetry editor of *The Offing*. She also teaches creative writing at Columbia University and co-curates the Poets With Attitude (PWA) reading series with Tommy Pico. With poet and performer Angel Nafis, she is The Other Black Girl Collective.

Of "Everything Will Be Taken Away," Parker writes: "I wrote this poem after reflecting on and being seduced by a text-based piece by conceptual artist Adrian Piper, from which the poem takes its title. In summer 2015, with death so ubiquitous on the news and in the air, the phrase resonated like a chant, a reminder, a comfort as well as an elegy. This is a poem about mourning the past and the future simultaneously. It's about understanding your own body as a terminal thing."

HAI-DANG PHAN was born in Vietnam in 1980. He came to the United States as a refugee with his family in 1982 and grew up in Wisconsin. He is the author of the chapbook *Small Wars* (Convulsive Editions, 2016). A graduate of the University of Florida's MFA program in creative writing, he lives in Des Moines and teaches at Grinnell College.

Of "My Father's 'Norton Introduction to Literature,' Third Edition (1981)," Hai-Dang Phan writes: "It's a failed essay. On first looking into my father's *Norton*, I wanted to write a personal essay exploring some of the same questions of migration, mourning, and inheritance in prose. However, the unreconstructed poet in me sabotaged the wannabe essayist from the start because what I did right away was make a list—which resists narrative and induces poetry—of all the words my father had marked for attention. That list, those charm-like words, cast their spell. And so the poem, and so the opening list. It's a found poem, artifice meets accident, sourced from the literary works and reader's notes of my father's textbook. I wanted to convey the uniquely tactile, sensuous, and material experience of reading and responding to a printed book, alongside the intimate thrill of handwriting. It's a poem-quilt made of well-worn texts (by, and in order of appearance: Emily Dickinson, Ernest Hemingway, Gabriel García Márquez, Robert Frost, John Crowe Ransom, and Wallace Stevens). It's the ghost of a sestina. 'It has the appearance of a sesqui-sestina,' a perceptive, trusted reader (the poem bears the fingerprints of a number of them) observed after reading a later, slightly longer draft. During early drafts I actually had the bad idea, quickly discarded, of using words from the list I compiled as my six end-words for a hypothetical sestina. The six-line stanza form I ultimately kept, for shape and restraint, recursiveness and sprawl. It's a capsule biography, a portrait of my father (who served during the war as an officer in the South Vietnamese Navy, mostly on a small patrol boat unit in the Mekong Delta); as an immigrant trying to learn the language and literature of his adopted country; as a father trying to come to terms with the loss of his first child, whom he only ever saw alive once, and while he was in reeducation camp. I feel compelled to note that it's my mother's grief, briefly acknowledged and secreted inside a borrowed metaphor, which haunts the margins of the poem when I return to it now. After all, she was the one who had to deal with the death of her daughter while her husband was imprisoned, her private sorrow its own prison house. It's also a self-portrait because my life is bound up with this family trauma, and the historical trauma surrounding it. Insofar as I grapple with these legacies, as a writer I'm interested in the formal problems and possibilities they pose. Given the intense emotional response my father's marginalia provoked in me and what became the concerns of the poem, I needed a distancing strategy to combat the threat of cheap sentiment, false immediacy, and unknowing appropriation. Hence, the professorial persona and voice of the detached academic. In October 2012, when I came across my father's *Norton* while visiting my parents in Wisconsin, I had just started teaching at Grinnell College and entered a period of uncertainty about the course of my writing life. It's a reconciliation between two selves, the poet and the professor, that I, too, often see as conflictual, not to mention the age-old wars between fathers and sons, the present and the past. It's my marginalia on his marginalia, a double-annotation and translation, of what words, memories, people, and events mean as they change contexts, of the unknowable. It's a record and reenactment of reading, between the lines, behind the words, for the lives we've missed, others' and our own."

ROWAN RICARDO PHILLIPS is the author of two books of poetry, *The Ground* (2012) and *Heaven* (2015), both published by Farrar, Straus and Giroux, as well as the collection of literary essays *When Blackness Rhymes with Blackness* (Dalkey Archive Press, 2010) and a translation, from the Catalan, of *Ariadne in the Grotesque Labyrinth* (Dalkey, 2012). He has received a Guggenheim Fellowship, a Whiting Writers' Award, the Pen/Joyce Osterweil Prize for Poetry, and the GLCA New Writers Award. His poetry has been translated into Catalan, German, Italian, Norwegian, and Spanish. He has taught at Harvard, Columbia, Princeton, and SUNY-Stony Brook University. A fellow of the New York Institute for the Humanities at NYU, he lives in New York City and Barcelona.

Phillips writes: "If I were to tell you that 'The First Last Light in the Sky' began as a short story, I would understand if you didn't believe me. It certainly doesn't read like, say, a poem by Browning or Frost, many of which you could be conned into thinking began as prose narratives. And that's intended no slight to their verses: after all, it's well known that Yeats would scratch out a paragraph or two about the mise-en-scène of a poem before the perfume of his prosody took over. Is Lydia Davis writing poetry? Is Haruki Murakami writing prose? Poetry is my resting state. And as I was editing this story (there was so much more of it you'll never see), the reductions began to distribute themselves into parcels of ten syllables with somewhat of an iambic temperament, the vision became prophetic instead of prosaic. I'm not one for grand statements about poetry but I take it as gospel that you should never run away from a poem when a poem declares its presence in your life. And so the short story that was became the poem that this now is. Its ending was not in the original, but as the poem made its presence clear it had words for me, like an annunciation—song and pain, it said. A bit of I AM THAT I AM. This is sung and seen in lala and 'aiai': mirror images of each other but for 'aiai,' the ancient wail of lament from myth, looking like a lala that's been cut clean through by something severe."

STANLEY PLUMLY was born in Barnesville, Ohio, in 1939. He is a Distinguished University Professor at the University of Maryland, College

Park, and a member of the American Academy of Arts & Sciences. From W. W. Norton, recent volumes of poems include *Old Heart* (2007; Los Angeles Times Book Prize, 2008) and *Orphan Hours* (2012). Recent books of prose include *Posthumous Keats: A Personal Biography* (2008) and *The Immortal Evening: A Legendary Dinner with Keats, Wordsworth, and Lamb* (2014; the Truman Capote Prize for Literary Criticism, 2015). He lives in Frederick, Maryland.

Of "Variation on a Line from Elizabeth Bishop's 'Five Flights Up,'" Plumly writes: "'Five Flights Up' is the last poem in Elizabeth Bishop's final single volume, *Geography III*. To me, it has always represented a kind of swan song of both exhaustion and reconciliation. It is an exquisitely beautiful exit poem. One reaches an age when even bending over to tie one's shoes becomes one more signature of mortality."

JAMES RICHARDSON was born in Bradenton, Florida, in 1950. His recent books include *During* (Copper Canyon Press, 2016), which was awarded the Poetry Society of America's Alice Fay Di Castagnola Prize, *By the Numbers: Poems and Aphorisms* (Copper Canyon, 2010), *Interglacial: New and Selected Poems and Aphorisms* (Ausable Press, 2004), and *Vectors: Aphorisms and Ten-Second Essays* (Ausable Press, 2001). He received the 2011 Jackson Poetry Prize. He has taught at Princeton University since 1980.

Of "Late Aubade," Richardson writes: "An aubade is a dawn song, often for the parting of lovers. So a *late* aubade would be faintly paradoxical, though of course I also mean late in *life*. My poem borrows from Hardy a little of his rhythm and his habit of writing self-elegies and Farewells to Life, not surprising in a poet who did much of his best work in his seventies and eighties. It reminds me a little of his 'He Never Expected Much.' Hard to say exactly who Hardy was addressing his good-byes to, but my Life is a woman who seems to be very old and very young at the same time."

PATRICK ROSAL is the author of four books of poetry, most recently *Brooklyn Antediluvian* (Persea Books, 2016). Other titles are *Boneshepherds* (2011), *My American Kundiman* (2006), and *Uprock Headspin Scramble and Dive* (2003), all from Persea Books. A former Fulbright research fellow, he is a full-time faculty member of the MFA program at Rutgers University–Camden.

Of "At the Tribunals," Rosal writes: "When I started reading and writing seriously, I was astonished by the lack of violence in American poetry. It's such a major part of our history and of almost every coming-of-age narrative for people on the margins, and yet much of our poetry seemed uninterested in looking squarely at this nation's violence. I feel I've inherited a tradition (which isn't solely literary) that asks me to examine the evidence of my own life and how I might have been complicit in America's brutishness. To me, it is a necessary exercise as a citizen and an artist. I don't think I needed headlines to teach me this. Early on in my writing life, I felt charged with this responsibility by elder storytellers, singers, gamblers, mga manghihilot, poets, and others. Imagine if young men were taught that sort of reflection—if they were given permission to be confounded by their own brutality rather than so simply assured of its power."

DAVID ST. JOHN was born in Fresno, California, in 1949. His books of poetry include *Study for the World's Body: New and Selected Poems* (1994); *The Auroras* (HarperCollins, 2012); and *The Window* (Arctos Press, 2014). A volume of his essays, reviews, and interviews is entitled *Where the Angels Come Toward Us* (White Pine Press, 1995). He has written libretti for Donald Crockett's opera based on his book *The Face*, and Frank Ticheli's choral symphony *The Shore*. He is the coeditor of *American Hybrid: A Norton Anthology of New Poetry* (2009) and has edited a posthumous collection of poems by Larry Levis, *The Darkening Trapeze: Last Poems* (Graywolf Press, 2016). He has received the Rome Fellowship and the award in literature from the American Academy of Arts and Letters; the O. B. Hardison Prize from the Folger Shakespeare Library; and the George Drury Smith Lifetime Achievement Award. He is professor and chair of English at the University of Southern California and lives in Venice Beach, California.

Of "Vineyard," St. John writes: "For most of 2012–2014, I wasn't writing my own poems at all. I was busy editing Larry Levis's book, *The Darkening Trapeze: Last Poems*, so it didn't really matter to me. It was wonderful to immerse myself in Larry's poems, as it had always been. Of course, I found myself thinking a lot of the times in the late 1960s when he and I were both living still in Fresno, and of the San Joaquin Valley with its acres of peach and fig, almond and apricot trees all blossoming every spring. And of the vineyards Larry grew up among. In those days, the land just north of our college was given over entirely to orchards, hard as it is to think of that now. I was thinking also of friends of mine, and friends of Larry's; some were about to go to Vietnam and some would be going north to Canada. The taste of that time has always seemed to me the taste of valley dust. As time passed, it became the taste of ash."

BRENDA SHAUGHNESSY was born in Okinawa, Japan, in 1970, and is currently associate professor of English at Rutgers University–Newark. Her books are *So Much Synth* (Copper Canyon Press, 2016), *Our Andromeda* (Copper Canyon, 2012), *Human Dark with Sugar* (Copper Canyon, 2008), and *Interior with Sudden Joy* (Farrar, Straus and Giroux, 1999). She lives with her husband, the poet Craig Morgan Teicher, and their two children in Verona, New Jersey.

Of "But I'm the Only One," Shaughnessy writes: "It occurred to me that I probably should have changed the names in this poem. They're all real names, real people—it all really happened pretty much this way. It's a kind of ambivalent love poem to that time in the mid-nineties in New York City where you got the *Village Voice* the minute it came out and went home immediately to get on your home phone and start calling about apartments, if you needed an apartment. And if your girlfriend of sixteen months or so dumped you and there you were dumping red wine on your broken heart in between shifts at Kinko's, you needed an apartment. Getting a room in the 'Dyke Loft' with three unknown roommates was a thread of hope, never mind the rent was out of my range—I was desperate to be chosen. When I was, I felt so incredibly cool. In the three years I lived there nine roommates cycled through, not including the cats. We had parties, we had troubles, and there's no doubt that in that Dyke Loft I became a poet. I wrote my first book there, in large part because I couldn't afford to do anything but stay home and write.

"I hope none of the women in this poem feel slighted or irritated by their appearance here. We were young together in an intense way, for a short while—it wasn't easy to be out back then; in too many ways it wasn't even safe—and we formed a strange, fierce, passionate circle. That loft was full of dreams. For all our differences, we could agree on certain lesbian anthems, be admitted gratis to the Clit Club on Friday nights, all huddle together to watch *Ellen* or 'the lesbian wedding episode' on *Friends*. Ours was a subculture, and we were working toward discovering who we were within it and, eventually, without it."

ANYA SILVER was born in Swarthmore, Pennsylvania, in 1968. She has published two books of poetry with the Louisiana State University Press, *The Ninety-Third Name of God* (2010) and *I Watched You Disappear*

(2014); her third book, *From Nothing*, will be published by LSU in 2016. She was named Georgia Author of the Year for Poetry in 2015. She is a professor of English at Mercer University in Macon, Georgia.

Silver writes: "Fairy tales were my introduction to literature, and I still remember sitting on my father's lap as he read to me from our big blue book of the Grimms' fairy tales. I hadn't remembered the fairy tale 'Maid Maleen' until I reread it for a fairy tale course that I was teaching. I was drawn to the tale's self-sufficient heroine, who manages to escape, with her maid, from the tower in which her father has imprisoned her. As is the case in many fairy tales, Maid Maleen is restored to her former status and happiness through marriage at the end of the story. Western fairy tales in general posit a benign universe that rewards kindness and humility. Painful events are merely erased by good fortune. However, as someone living with metastatic breast cancer, I am no longer able to accept such a view of the world. The deaths of my friends remain with me. I can't forget, and don't want to forget, their suffering, or the fact that approximately forty thousand women and men will die of breast cancer each year. I reject pink ribbon culture and the false narrative of breast cancer as a curable disease that has been perpetuated by prominent organizations. Women with metastatic breast cancer know that there is 'never safety again.' The smoke of our beloveds' cremated bodies 'remains forever' in our lungs. I wanted the poem to capture, through mythological imagery, the emotional burden of loss.

"Fairy tales abide with us because they can be interpreted and reinterpreted in ways that suit our personal and cultural needs. It's not necessary for a reader to read 'Maid Maleen' as a poem about breast cancer. The poem addresses trauma of any kind. I wrote it primarily about my own disease, but imagery from the Holocaust and Stalin's Great Terror also informed my choices. The line 'There will be no wedding today' is from my favorite fairy tale, *Jane Eyre*. #metavivor"

TAIJE SILVERMAN was born in San Francisco in 1974. Her first book, *Houses Are Fields*, was published in 2009 by Louisiana State University Press. She has received the 2016 Anne Halley Prize from *The Massachusetts Review*, the 2010–11 W.K. Rose Fellowship from Vassar College, the Emory University Poetry Fellowship, and several residencies at the MacDowell Colony as well as from the Virginia Center for the Creative Arts. In 2010–11, she taught at the University of Bologna as a Fulbright Scholar. She now teaches at the University of Pennsylvania.

Of "Grief," Silverman writes: "Two months before the Mother's

Day on which I wrote this poem, I had given birth to my son, and the grief I felt for my mother's absence was lined with his presence. I felt both that she was more here, in my motherhood, and that he was less here, for the fact that she couldn't know him. A limbo—like the limbo he must have entered between being in my womb and being in the world. I'd been holding him in my arms outside the neighborhood community center when this rush of maple seeds came gusting around us, and I wondered what he must think of them, this sudden whirling of something he had no name or context for. Grief is like that, too. The impulse is to name it, to put a measure on what's been lost, but the completeness of the loss is as unknowable as the helicopter seeds must have seemed to my baby who had no words. And missing my mother as I sat down to write this, I was glad for that mystery. Who knows what's here and what isn't, or how much stays in the in-between."

TOM SLEIGH's books include *Station Zed*, *Army Cats* (Graywolf Press, 2015 and 2011), winner of the John Updike Award from the American Academy of Arts and Letters, and *Space Walk*, winner of the $100,000 Kingsley Tufts Poetry Award. His work appears in *The Best of the Best American Poetry*. He has received the Shelley Prize from the Poetry Society of America, and awards from the American Academy in Berlin, Civitella Ranieri, the Lila Wallace Fund, the Guggenheim Foundation, and the National Endowment for the Arts. He teaches at Hunter College and works as a journalist in the Middle East and Africa.

Of "Prayer for Recovery," Sleigh writes: "When I was living in Berlin a few years ago, I often visited the Topography of Terror Museum dedicated to the history of the Gestapo and SS. It's housed in a new building on the same site as the former headquarters of both the Gestapo and SS. To visit the museum is to understand the Nazi mania for documentation: thousands of photographs from the era are mounted throughout the exhibition space and explained with terse, accurate, and unflinching descriptions of what happened.

"A photograph I came back to again and again, one of the most troubling and moving, was of August Landmesser, a trade unionist, present at a Nazi rally to celebrate the launch of a ship he'd helped build, the SSS *Horst Wessel*. In the photo, Landmesser is surrounded by thousands and thousands of heiling citizens, their right arms shooting out in epileptic abandon, their mouths shouting 'Sieg Heil' as Hitler shouts 'Sieg Heil' back. But alone among the vast throng, Landmesser refuses to give the Nazi salute; instead, he stands there with his arms resolutely folded, looking a little disgusted, a little dismayed by his fellow Germans.

"His story is a love story of sorts: he joined the Party in 1931, hoping to get work, but fell in love with a Jewish woman, Irma Eckler. Not only was he expelled from the Party, he was unable to marry her because of the Nuremberg racial laws passed in 1935. They had a baby girl, anyway—and then the full logic of Naziism caught up to them. They refused to hide their relationship in public, and had another child. So he was imprisoned, released, imprisoned again in a concentration camp, released again, then forced into a penal infantry unit consisting of thousands of other prisoners, and died in Croatia six months before Germany surrendered. Shuttled among concentration camps, his wife eventually died in the Bernburg Euthanasia Centre in 1942.

"Somehow their children survived the war, one in the care of Irma's mother, the other with foster parents.

"All this is to say that the poem came out of a stay in a Berlin hospital, and while I was in my room, in between worrying about my blood counts, I often thought of Landmesser standing there all alone, in radically different historical conditions, not exactly pure because of his former Party affiliation, but also a man of courage. I'd stare at my IV bag and watch the drip, or I'd walk in the hallways clinging to my IV pole, passing through the electric eye that opened the door from one wing to another, and I'd think of Landmesser scowling, solitary—and at the moment the photo was taken at least, almost suicidally brave. The electric eye also haunted me, as if the door automatically swinging back opened onto another dimension where people like Landmesser and me could meet.

"The poem suggests that some state of us, which of course we can't know, will live on after us, just as Landmesser has lived on in a photograph that he never saw or even knew was being taken.

"And since he was a shipyard worker, he would have known how to use a rivet gun."

A. E. STALLINGS, born in 1968, is an American poet who has lived in Greece since 1999. She grew up in Decatur, Georgia, and studied classics at the University of Georgia and later at Oxford University. She has published three poetry collections, most recently *Olives* (TriQuarterly Books, 2012). Her verse translation of Lucretius, *The Nature of Things*, is available from Penguin Classics (2007), and a translation of Hesiod's *Works and Days* is forthcoming.

Of "Alice, Bewildered," Stallings writes: "I have always identified with Alice—partly, no doubt, because Alicia (that's what 'A.' stands for) is a diminutive of Alice; Alice is also my mother's name. We had a two-record LP set of a complete and unabridged reading of *Alice in Wonderland* when I was a child (which has since been thrown out, unfortunately), by some British actor, with interludes of woodwind music, and I used to listen to it over and over, particularly when I was ill. It's the narrative soundtrack for me of fever and being half asleep in the middle of the day in a dim room; a comforting soundtrack, the aural equivalent of alphabet soup and saltine crackers. I probably know swaths of it verbatim.

"*Through the Looking Glass* is a different matter—that book I know from reading rather than listening, and it strikes me as a more grown-up and cerebral book. If *Alice in Wonderland* is dreamy, there's something of the nightmare about *Through the Looking Glass*. I know it in a more partial way, say, the relevant passage on Humpty Dumpty and literary theory. Rereading it (or was I reading it to my son?), I was struck afresh with the disturbing passage about the Wood Where Things Have No Names. Even though Alice falls down the rabbit hole in *Alice in Wonderland*, there is a sense of absurd adventure to it. *Through the Looking Glass* feels more of a katabasis, a journey to the underworld; indeed the forest of forgetfulness puts one a bit in mind of Dante, or Virgil. It makes sense that Alice thinks her name might begin with 'L'—'Lacie' was Charles Dodgson's anagram for Alice, and in the name 'Alice' one could almost feel that the 'A' is a privative 'a.' In Greek, Alice (and Alicia) is 'Aliki' or 'Alike.' So when I reread that passage, a sort of queasy chill went through me, and I wanted to explore that moment, to be Alice when she loses who she is."

FRANK STANFORD, born in Mississippi in 1948, was a prolific poet who has been called one of the great voices of death. He wrote ten volumes of poetry and a collection of short stories: *The Singing Knives* (1971), *Ladies from Hell* (1974), *Field Talk* (1974), *Shade* (1975), *Arkansas Bench Stone* (1975), *Constant Stranger* (1976), *The Battlefield Where the Moon Says I Love You* (1977), *Crib Death* (1978), *You* (1979), *The Light the Dead See* (1991), and *Conditions Uncertain and Likely to Pass Away* (1990). 2015 saw the publication of two new volumes: *What About This: Collected Poems of Frank Stanford* (Copper Canyon Press, edited by Michael Wiegers) and *Hidden Water: From the Frank Stanford Archives* (Third Man Books, eds. Michael Wiegers and Chet Weise). Stanford worked as a land surveyor and spent most of his life in Arkansas. He died in 1978.

Of "Cotton You Lose in the Field," Michael Wiegers writes: "When I began the long task of compiling and editing *What About This: Collected Poems of Frank Stanford*, the poet C. D. Wright shared with me several unpublished manuscripts and encouraged me to visit the Beinecke Library at Yale, which had recently acquired many of his papers. This poem comes from a manuscript, *Plain Songs*, which claims the poet Jean Follain as an influence and prominently features Stanford's 'versions'—mock translations—and original poems seasoned by his explorations of poetry in other languages. And yet, despite an international influence, this poem remains thoroughly autochthonous in its voice and demeanor."

SUSAN STEWART was born in York, Pennsylvania, in 1952. She is the author of six books of poems: *Yellow Stars and Ice* (Princeton University Press, 1981); *The Hive* (University of Georgia Press, 1987); *The Forest* (University of Chicago Press, 1995); *Columbarium* (Chicago, 2003); *Red Rover* (Chicago, 2008); and the forthcoming *Cinder* (Graywolf Press, 2017). *Columbarium* won the National Book Critics Circle Award in 2004. She is the Avalon Foundation University Professor in the Humanities at Princeton University. A former MacArthur Fellow and Chancellor of the Academy of American Poets, she is a member of the American Academy of Arts and Sciences. Her translations include *Love Lessons: Selected Poems of Alda Merini* (Princeton University Press, 2009) and a cotranslation of *Milo De Angelis: Theme of Farewell and After-Poems* (Chicago, 2013), and her prose works include *Poetry and the Fate of the Senses* (2002) and *The Poet's Freedom* (2011), both from Chicago. She has been a fellow of the American Academy in Berlin and in the summer of 2016 was visiting professor at the Université Paris VII/Diderot.

Of "What Piranesi Knew," Stewart writes: "This brief poem is an appreciation of the mysterious *carceri*, or 'prisons,' etchings of the great eighteenth-century Venetian and Roman print-maker Giovanni Battista Piranesi. These etchings have been important to English-speaking writers and artists since they first appeared in 1750. I have been studying them for many years, trying to grasp Piranesi's remarkable sense of space and shadows. My fascination with his work and life began during a period when I often taught in Rome and has sent me to study print-making in recent years at the Pennsylvania Academy— the wonderful art school in my home town of Philadelphia. But in this poem, I have tried to express an emotional connection to his prints, above all."

NOMI STONE was born in Los Angeles in 1981. She is the author of the poetry collection *Stranger's Notebook* (TriQuarterly Books, 2008), an MFA candidate in poetry at Warren Wilson, and a PhD candidate in cultural anthropology at Columbia. She has a master's in Middle Eastern Studies from Oxford and was a Fulbright Scholar in creative writing in Tunisia. She is working on *Kill Class*, a collection of poems based on two years of ethnographic fieldwork conducted within combat simulations in mock Middle Eastern villages erected by the U.S. military across America.

Stone writes: "Here are his hands, moving precisely over the silent bed of static, trembling like two birds in formation over the city. In 'Drones: An Exercise in Awe-Terror,' the Hellfire missile hatches in the pilot's mind as his hands render the fate of a faraway landscape. He produces the spectacle he watches at a distance while it ripples into his interior space. I wrote this poem while doing my PhD coursework in anthropology at Columbia University. I was taking a class with Marilyn Ivy on theories of the 'Sublime.' No class in my life has ever moved or unsettled me more. We read Longinus, Edmund Burke, Kant, Adorno, and others about the relationship between the body and the senses to awe and terror, to safety and harm. We interrogated Enlightenment texts that contained or domesticated that awe-terror through 'Reason.' Together in that room, we considered the vibration of the soul when confronted by an object in the world that creates vertigo, that makes the ego cave in. We spoke about the sublime of mountains and oceans. We spoke about death and God.

"This poem is my attempt to enact and grapple with these theories of awe-terror in wartime. When I wrote the poem, I was inspired in particular by a 2010 *Frontline* documentary, 'Digital Nation,' and a series of interviews my dear friend Caitlin McNally did with drone pilots to try to access their sensory and interior experiences. In the ensuing years, I conducted two years of my own ethnographic fieldwork with military personnel within pre-deployment trainings and interviewed many soldiers about their experiences of the perceived adversary. The poems inspired by that fieldwork constitute *Kill Class*, my collection in progress. In this poem, I am trying to represent the American military attempt to contain what is imagined as an ever-permutating adversary as well as the erasure of those individuals' humanness when they are turned into coordinates. But most especially, I am interested in the potential of the moment's gravity yawning open: the pilot's recognition that: 'They // told me there is a place like / that, and I am actually in / it (changing / it) (right now).' The first two sections of the poem ('The Imagination Cannot' and 'When Reason Came') are based on the theories of Kant, and the third section ('Black') is based on the theories of Adorno. I seek here, through tools of form like sonic and syntax, to gesture toward the impossibility of representation amid the experience of awe and terror: the metaphor flails toward an object that can't be captured. Language breaks down. We are all implicated. Blackout."

ADRIENNE SU, born in Atlanta in 1967 and raised there, is the author of four books of poems: *Living Quarters* (Manic D Press, 2015), *Having None of It* (Manic D Press, 2012), *Sanctuary* (Manic D Press, 2006), and *Middle Kingdom* (Alice James Books, 1997). "Peaches" comes from her current project, which seeks to remember the Chinese Americans of Atlanta in the 1970s and 1980s, often through food. Su received a National Endowment for the Arts fellowship in poetry in 2007 and has taught at Dickinson College in Carlisle, Pennsylvania, since 2000.

Of "Peaches," Su writes: "In Atlanta a few decades ago, buying an abundance of peaches in season should have been as Georgian as it gets. It didn't require the consumer to travel with as few clothes as possible so as to fill every suitcase with food, as my parents used to do on returning from any city with a Chinatown. And unlike shrimp fried with their heads still on, or braised pigs' ears, peaches didn't scare the neighbors. Thus, in my childhood, peaches in quantity seemed a sign of my family's successful assimilation, versus the many markers of our foreignness. Asians were a tiny minority in Georgia then, so small that when I chanced to meet any, I figured—often correctly—that my parents already knew them.

"Much later, I realized that even a crate of ripe peaches stood out in suburban Atlanta. I also learned that the peach tree, after which many downtown Atlanta streets are named, is native to China. In retrospect, many of the foods I once simplistically categorized as Chinese, American, or Southern have much more ambiguous origins. Exploring them in my writing has become a way of understanding the place from which I came and appreciating the people who shaped it.

"Having imitated my parents and moved to where the academic employment is, I now live in central Pennsylvania, where the shrimp have no heads and small farms thrive. Though Asian ingredients can be hard to find, the region is a fertile playground for a cook. Of course

I can never resist summer's peaches by the crate. Meanwhile, Atlanta, remade by an influx of new immigrants, has become the city from which I routinely bring a suitcase full of food."

JAMES TATE (1943–2015) was born in Kansas City, Missouri, and studied at Kansas State College of Pittsburgh and the Iowa Writers' Workshop, where he received an MFA. His first collection of poems, *The Lost Pilot* (1967), was selected for the Yale Series of Younger Poets; he would go on to receive the 1992 Pulitzer Prize and the Poetry Society of America's William Carlos Williams Award for his *Selected Poems* and the 1994 National Book Award for *Worshipful Company of Fletchers*. He also won fellowships from the National Endowment for the Arts and the Guggenheim Foundation, and the Wallace Stevens Award from the Academy of American Poets. He was the guest editor of *The Best American Poetry 1997*. In his introduction to that volume he wrote, "In my experience poets are not different from other people. You have your dullards, your maniacs, your mild eccentrics, etc. Except for this one thing they do—write poems. And in this they are singularly strange. They may end up with an audience and a following of some sort, but in truth they write their poems with various degrees of obsessiveness mostly for themselves, for the pleasure and satisfaction it gives them. And for the hunger and need nothing else can abate."

Tate was married to the poet Dara Wier. He taught at the University of Massachusetts at Amherst for more than forty years. His recent books include *The Eternal Ones of the Dream: Selected Poems 1990–2010* (2012), *The Ghost Soldiers* (2008), and *Return to the City of White Donkeys* (2004), all from Ecco Press, and *Dreams of a Robot Dancing Bee: 44 Stories* (Verse Press, 2002; Wave Books, 2008). John Ashbery described Tate as "the poet of possibilities, of morph, of surprising consequences, lovely or disastrous." In a *Paris Review* interview with Charles Simic, Tate said, "I like to start with the ordinary, and then nudge it, and then think, 'What happens next, what happens next?'"

Dara Wier writes: "The title for the poem, 'Dome of the Hidden Temple,' is the poem's original and only title. When the time came to decide on a book title *Dome of the Hidden Temple* became one of the strongest contenders. Emily Pettit worked with Jim to winnow down the number of poems he wanted included in *Dome of the Hidden Pavilion* (Ecco, 2015), which turned out to be his last book—which I'm sure he didn't feel to be his last book—before his death in July 2015. He left behind over 300 new poems written since *Dome of the Hidden Pavilion* was made. To the best of my memory Jim indicated he felt 'temple' was a little too Indiana Jones for a book title while just fine for a single poem title."

LEE UPTON was born in St. Johns, Michigan, in 1953. Her sixth book of poetry, *Bottle the Bottles the Bottles the Bottles*, appeared from the Cleveland State University Poetry Center in 2015. Her collection of short stories, *The Tao of Humiliation* (BOA Editions), was named one of the "best books of 2014" by *Kirkus Reviews*. She is the Francis A. March Professor of English at Lafayette College.

Of "The Apology," Upton writes: "How can we not yearn to describe nature and to identify with the natural world, given that we're part of that world? We've despoiled so much of the natural world, and yet we feel summoned to describe nature relentlessly, while nature with its peculiar power defies description. Always we hit up against a limit when we see all nature as defined by human nature—not that such a tendency has ever stopped some of us from enjoying the way we're summoned to language by natural beauty. On another level, if 'it was asking for it,' nature not only invokes our yearning for description but asks for its own survival. 'It' asks for 'it'—all of itself, if not less of us."

C. K. WILLIAMS (1936–2015)—Charles Kenneth Williams on official transcripts, Charlie to his friends—grew up in New Jersey and played college basketball before transferring to the University of Pennsylvania, where he studied philosophy and English. He graduated in 1959. He began writing verse when a girlfriend asked him to write a poem, and Houghton Mifflin published his first collection, *Lies*, on Anne Sexton's recommendation, ten years later. He met his wife, Catherine, a French jeweler, in 1973 at an airline ticket counter when their flight was delayed. Known for his signature long lines in verse, Williams translated plays and wrote critical essays, the latter collected in *Poetry and Consciousness* (1998). The author of twenty-two books of poetry, Williams received a Guggenheim Fellowship, a National Book Award, a Pulitzer Prize, and a grant from the National Endowment for the Arts. *Flesh and Blood* won the National Book Critics Circle Award; *Repair* won the Pulitzer Prize in poetry and the Los Angeles Times Book Prize; and *The Singing* won the National Book Award. He wrote a critical study, *On Whitman*; a memoir, *Misgivings*; and two books of essays, *Poetry and Consciousness* and *In Time: Poets, Poems, and the Rest*. His most recent books include *Collected Poems* (2006), *Wait* (2010), *All at Once: Prose*

Poems (2014), and *Selected Later Poems* (2015), all from Farrar, Straus and Giroux. He also published two children's books, *How the Nobble Was Finally Found*, and *A Not Scary Story About Big Scary Things*, both from Houghton Mifflin Harcourt.

Williams divided his time between Paris and Princeton, where he taught. Robert Pinsky wrote, "His fearless inventions, with their big long lines, quest after the entirety of life: he will include every emotion, every bit of evidence that has a natural claim on our attention. Contemporary life is so rich and vivid in his poetry that by contrast many of the movies and poems we are used to seem pale, spaced-out and insipid." Williams once observed, "For a long time I had been writing poetry that leaves everything out. It's like a code. You say very little and send it out to people who know how to decode it. But then I realized that by writing longer lines and longer poems I could actually write the way I thought and the way I felt. I wanted to enter areas given over to prose writers, I wanted to talk about things the way a journalist can talk about things, but in poetry, not prose." In a *Los Angeles Times* interview, Williams remarked that "the drama of American poetry is based very much on experience. It's coming out of all the different cultures. We're an enormous nation and we have an enormous poetry."

ELEANOR WILNER was born in Cleveland, Ohio, in 1937. She has published seven books of poetry, most recently *Tourist in Hell* (University of Chicago Press, 2010) and *The Girl with Bees in Her Hair* (Copper Canyon Press, 2004); she coedited with Maurice Manning *The Rag-Picker's Guide to Poetry: Poems, Poets, Process* (University of Michigan Press, 2013). She has been awarded fellowships from the MacArthur Foundation, National Endowment for the Arts, and Pennsylvania Council on the Arts. She teaches in the MFA Program for Writers at Warren Wilson College.

Of "To Think of How Cold," Wilner writes: "Sometimes a line lingers in the memory over many years. Such a line, first encountered over forty years ago, was Emily Brontë's 'Cold in the earth—and the deep snow piled above thee . . . ' What the line reveals, it seems to me, is how the imagination, whose envisioning and transformative powers seem boundless, nevertheless cannot imagine non-being. This is the horror that the line catches, and my poem enacts: to imagine a person in the grave as if such cold could be felt brings our sentient life to one who is loved and gone . . . and herein, helplessly, lies more grief.

"One of the joyous experiences of my life was attending a Brahmin cremation in Bali, the body burned in the flaming effigy of a bull, its visible destruction and its release in fire to the air, the ashes carried afterward to be scattered at sunset in the sea—it is this, perhaps, among other things, that feeds the jubilant way the poem turns when Lear speaks. The poem, to fully unfold, does demand a knowledge of *King Lear*, but so, to my mind, does life."

Mississippi-born (1939) with a Michigan finish, former California poet laureate AL YOUNG is the author of twenty-five books, including poem collections, novels, and memoirs. He has received the Wallace Stegner, Guggenheim, Fulbright, and Woodrow Wilson fellowships and has taught writing and literature at Stanford, Berkeley, Santa Cruz, Davis, the University of Michigan, Bennington College, and Davidson College. He is Distinguished Professor at California College of the Arts' MFA in writing program in San Francisco.

Of "The Drummer Omar: Poet of Percussion," Young writes: "I composed this poem-tribute to the great drummer Omar Clay in 2008, the same year he died on us. Loved or enlivened by lovers of jazz and pop music all over the world, Omar's complex yet mindful personality walked and talked. Like today's tempered steel drum, fabled drums of West Africa were vocally tuned. Across respectable miles, we could hear and talk to one another. Time. Space-Time. Omar, an elder, had made his way to the University of Michigan's School of Music by the time I got there in 1957. He had fathered a daughter and was devoted to her care and upbringing. We kept meeting around campus. Omar was attending school and drumming with Ann Arbor's and Detroit's star musicians. I was learning guitar, performing folk songs and blues, coediting *Generation*, the campus inter-arts journal, and drifting cross genre. I remember a certain sunny Ann Arbor spring afternoon, a Saturday. He'd dropped by to hang for a minute. We'd been listening to Sonny Rollins's 'Airegin' (Nigeria spelled backward), then switched to Billie Holiday of the 1930s (those stubborn old cuts, now Columbia classics—'Me, Myself and I,' 'A Sailboat in the Moonlight,' 'What a Little Moonlight Can Do'—loved-up with scratches). Omar said: 'You like this old shit, don't you?' He didn't say it in a judgmental way; he just said it. We ˙ ˙ ˙ hed. He'd come to my gigs and I to his. Omar and pianist-trumpeter ˙ ˙ ˙ es put a band together. The two of them ended up working ˙ ˙ ˙ lly with singer Sarah Vaughn. Later, while I was auditioning ˙ ˙ ˙ he place, Omar would show up. Never will I forget the ˙ ˙ ˙ at the Showcase when Charles Mingus was testing out bass players and drummers. Ron Carter was there that night. Omar showed up with a little pennywhistle he'd tweet at the end of one of his impeccable drum press-rolls. Once the eye-rolling Mingus tired of this, he reached out and snatched the whistle from Omar's hand. 'Mingus,' Omar had said to me before going onstage. 'Nut music.' We both then drifted to the San Francisco Bay Area, making it home. All I tried to do in the poem, a sonnet, was capture in Zen brushstrokes the magnificent splash of our relationship. I dedicate this comment to Barbara Chew, whose loving presence in drummer-golfer Omar Clay's life remains indelible."

MAGAZINES WHERE THE POEMS
WERE FIRST PUBLISHED

32 Poems, ed. George David Clark; associate eds. Nick McRae, Matt Morton, Sarah Rose Nordgren, and Michael Shewmaker. Washington & Jefferson College, Department of English, 60 S. Lincoln Street, Washington, PA 15301. www.32poems.com

The Academy of American Poets, Poem-a-Day, ed. Alex Dimitrov. www.poets.org

Alaska Quarterly Review, editor-in-chief Ronald Spatz. University of Alaska Anchorage, 3211 Providence Drive, Anchorage, AK 99508. www.uaa.alaska.edu/aqr

American Poets, ed. Alex Dimitrov; director of content Mary Gannon. www.poets.org/american-poets-magazine/home

The American Poetry Review, eds. David Bonanno and Elizabeth Scanlon. 320 S. Broad St., Hamilton #313, Philadelphia, PA 19102. www.aprweb.org

Birmingham Poetry Review, editor-in-chief Adam Vines; features ed. Gregory Fraser. 1720 2nd Avenue South, HB 203, Birmingham, AL 35294-1260.

Boston Review, poetry eds. Timothy Donnelly, Barbara Fischer, and Stefania Heim. bostonreview.net

Brilliant Corners, ed. Sascha Feinstein. Lycoming College, 700 College Place, Williamsport, PA 17701. www.lycoming.edu/brilliantCorners

Cherry Tree, ed. Jehanne Dubrow. www.washcoll.edu/centers/lithouse/cherry-tree

The Common, poetry ed. John Hennessy. www.thecommononline.org

Connotation Press, poetry ed. Julie Brooks Barbour. www.connotationpress.com

Copper Nickel, ed. Wayne Miller; poetry eds. Brian Barker and Nicky Beer. copper-nickel.org

Crab Orchard Review, poetry ed. Allison Joseph. Department of English, Faner Hall 2380, Mail Code 4503, Southern Illinois University Carbondale, 1000 Faner Drive, Carbondale, IL 62901. craborchardreview.siu.edu

The Georgia Review, ed. Stephen Corey. Main Library, Room 706A, 320 S. Jackson St., The University of Georgia, Athens, GA 30602-9009. garev.uga.edu

The Gettysburg Review, ed. Mark Drew. Gettysburg College, Gettysburg, PA 17325-1491. www.gettysburgreview.com

Green Mountains Review, poetry ed. Elizabeth Powell. greenmountains review.com

The Greensboro Review, poetry ed. Mackenzie Connellee. MFA Writing Program, 3302 MHRA Building, UNC-Greensboro, Greensboro, NC 27402-6170. tgronline.net

Gulf Coast, poetry eds. Luisa Muradyan, Erika Jo Brown, and Henk Rossouw. Department of English, University of Houston, 4800 Calhoun Road, Houston, TX 77204-3013. gulfcoastmag.org

Harvard Review, poetry ed. Major Jackson. Lamont Library, Harvard University, Cambridge, MA 02138. harvardreview.fas.harvard.edu

Hinchas de Poesía, poetry ed. Jim Heavily; guest editor James Cervantes. www.hinchasdepoesia.com

Image, ed. Gregory Wolfe. 3307 Third Avenue West, Seattle, WA 98119. imagejournal.org

jubilat, eds. Kevin González and Caryl Pagel; executive ed. Emily Pettit. www.jubilat.org

The Literary Review, poetry eds. Craig Morgan Teicher and Michael Morse. www.theliteraryreview.org

London Review of Books, poetry ed. Nick Richardson. www.lrb.co.uk

Los Angeles Review of Books, poetry ed. Elizabeth Metzger. lareviewof books.org

The Massachusetts Review, poetry eds. Ellen Doré Watson and Deborah Gorlin. Photo Lab 309, 211 Hicks Way, University of Massachusetts, Amherst, MA 01003. www.massreview.org

Miramar, ed. Christopher Buckley. 342 Oliver Road, Santa Barbara, CA 93109. www.miramarmagazine.org

New England Review, poetry ed. Rick Barot. www.nereview.com

New Letters, ed. Robert Stewart. University of Missouri–Kansas City, University House, 5101 Rockhill Rd., Kansas City, MO 64110. www.newletters.org

New Ohio Review, poetry ed. Jill Rosser. English Dept. 360 Ellis Hall, Ohio University, Athens, OH 5701. www.ohio.edu/nor

The New Yorker, poetry ed. Paul Muldoon. www.newyorker.com

The New York Times Magazine, poetry ed. for 2015, Natasha Trethewey. www.nytimes.com/column/magazine-poem

Paperbag, eds. Cathy Linh Che, Margarita Delcheva, Peter Moysaenko, Levi Rubeck, and Michael Vizsolyi. paperbagazine.com

The Paris Review, poetry ed. Robyn Creswell. 544 W. 27th St., New York, NY 10001. www.theparisreview.org

Parnassus, editor and publisher Herbert Leibowitz; co-editor Ben Downing. 205 W. 89th St. #8F, New York, NY 10024. parnassus review.com

Ploughshares, poetry ed. John Skoyles. www.pshares.org

Poetry, ed. Don Share. www.poetryfoundation.org

Poetry Daily, eds. Diane Boller and Don Selby. www.poems.com

Prairie Schooner, editor-in-chief Kwame Dawes; poetry eds. Arden Eli Hill and Rebecca Macijeski. 123 Andrews Hall, Lincoln, NE 68588-0334. prairieschooner.unl.edu

Ragazine, poetry ed. Emily Vogel. ragazine.cc

Raritan, editor in chief Jackson Lears. 31 Mine St., New Brunswick, NJ 08901. raritanquarterly.rutgers.edu

River Styx, ed. Richard Newman. 3139A South Grand Boulevard, Suite 203, St. Louis, MO 63118. www.riverstyx.org

The Southern Review, poetry ed. Jessica Faust. 338 Johnston Hall, Baton Rouge, LA 70803. thesouthernreview.org

Subtropics, poetry ed. Sidney Wade. subtropics.english.ufl.edu

Sycamore Review, poetry eds. Julie Henson and Emily Skaja; asst. poetry ed. Rachel Reynolds. sycamorereview.com

Tahoma Literary Review, poetry ed. and publisher Kelly Davio. tahoma literaryreview.com

Tin House, poetry ed. Matthew Dickman. www.tinhouse.com/home

Valley Voices, ed. John Zheng. libguides.mvsu.edu/valley-voices

Virginia Quarterly Review, www.vqronline.org

Waxwing, poetry eds. Justin Bigos and W. Todd Kaneko. waxwingmag .org

The Yale Review, ed. J. D. McClatchy. Yale University, PO Box 208243, New Haven, CT 06520-8243. yalereview.yale.edu

ACKNOWLEDGMENTS

The series editor thanks Mark Bibbins for his invaluable assistance. Warm thanks go also to Danielle Chin, Amy Gerstler, Ron Horning, Stacey Harwood, Sam O'Hana, and Mitch Sisskind; to Glen Hartley and Lynn Chu of Writers' Representatives; and to Ashley Gilliam, David Stanford Burr, Daniel Cuddy, Erich Hobbing, and Jessica Yu at Scribner.

Grateful acknowledgment is made of the magazines in which these poems first appeared and the magazine editors who selected them. A sincere attempt has been made to locate all copyright holders. Unless otherwise noted, copyright to the poems is held by the individual poets.

Christopher Bakken, "Sentence" from *Birmingham Poetry Review*. Reprinted by permission of the poet.

Catherine Barnett, "O Esperanza!" from *Tin House*. Reprinted by permission of the poet.

Rick Barot, "Whitman, 1841" from *Waxwing*. Reprinted by permission of the poet.

Jill Bialosky, "Daylight Savings" from *The Players*. © 2015 by Jill Bialosky. Reprinted by permission of the poet. Alfred A. Knopf, a division of Random House LLC. Also appeared in *Harvard Review*.

Paula Bohince, "Fruits de Mer" from *Parnassus*. Reprinted by permission of the poet.

Michelle Boisseau, "Ugglig" from *Among the Gorgons*. © 2016 by Michelle Boisseau. Reprinted by permission of Tampa Review Press. Also appeared in *The Gettysburg Review*.

Marianne Boruch, "I Get to Float Invisible" from *The Georgia Review*. Reprinted by permission of the poet.

David Bottoms, "Hubert Blankenship" from *The Southern Review*. Reprinted by permission of the poet.

Joseph Chapman and Laura Eve Engel, "32 Fantasy Football Teams" from *32 Poems*. Reprinted by permission of the poets.

Michael Collier, "Last Morning with Steve Orlen" from *The Greensboro Review*. Reprinted by permission of the poet.

Allison Davis, "The Heart of It All + A Free Beer" from *Sycamore Review*. Reprinted by permission of the poet.

Olena Kalytiak Davis, "On the Certainty of Bryan" from *Alaska Quarterly Review*. Reprinted by permission of the poet.

Natalie Diaz, "How the Milky Way Was Made" from *American Poets*. Reprinted by permission of the poet.

Denise Duhamel, "Humanity 101" from *The Southern Review*. Reprinted by permission of the poet.

Lynn Emanuel, "My Life" from *The New York Times Magazine*. Reprinted by permission of the poet.

Claudia Emerson, "Cyst" from *Impossible Bottle*. Reprinted by permission of Louisiana State University Press. Also appeared in *Subtropics*.

Martín Espada, "Here I Am" from *The American Poetry Review*. Reprinted by permission of the poet.

Peter Everwine, "The Kiskiminetas River" from *The Southern Review*. Reprinted by permission of the poet.

Alexis Rhone Fancher, "When I turned fourteen, my mother's sister took me to lunch and said:" from *Ragazine*. Reprinted by permission of the poet.

Charles Fort, "One Had Lived in a Room and Loved Nothing" from *Green Mountains Review*. Reprinted by permission of the poet.

Emily Fragos, "The Sadness of Clothes" from The Academy of American Poets' Poem-a-Day series. Reprinted by permission of the poet.

Amy Gerstler, "A Drop of Seawater Under the Microscope" from *Valley Voices*. Reprinted by permission of the poet.

Dana Gioia, "Meet Me at the Lighthouse" from *Virginia Quarterly Review*. Reprinted by permission of the poet.

Jorie Graham, "Reading to My Father" from *Boston Review*. Reprinted by permission of the poet.

Juliana Gray, "The Lady Responds" from *River Styx*. Reprinted by permission of the poet.

Linda Gregerson, "Font" from *Prodigal: New and Selected Poems 1976–2014*. © 2015 by Linda Gregerson. Reprinted by permission of Houghton Mifflin Harcourt. Also appeared in *Raritan*.

Jennifer Grotz, "Self-Portrait on the Street of an Unnamed Foreign City" from *Window Left Open*. © 2016 by Jennifer Grotz. Reprinted by permission of The Permissions Company, Inc., on behalf of Graywolf Press. Also appeared in the Academy of American Poets' Poem-a-Day series.

Brenda Shaughnessy, "But I'm the Only One" from *The Literary Review*. Reprinted by permission of the poet.

Anya Silver, "Maid Maleen" from *Harvard Review*. Reprinted by permission of the poet.

Taije Silverman, "Grief" from *The Massachusetts Review*. Reprinted by permission of the poet.

Tom Sleigh, "Prayer for Recovery" from *Station Zed*. © 2015 by Tom Sleigh. Reprinted by permission of The Permissions Company, Inc., on behalf of Graywolf Press. Also appeared in *Raritan*.

A. E. Stallings, "Alice, Bewildered" from *Virginia Quarterly Review*. Reprinted by permission of the poet.

Frank Stanford, "Cotton You Lose in the Field" from *What About This: Collected Poems of Frank Stanford*. Reprinted by permission of The Permissions Company, Inc., on behalf of Copper Canyon Press. Also appeared in The Academy of American Poets' Poem-a-Day series.

Susan Stewart, "What Piranesi Knew" from *The Paris Review*. Reprinted by permission of the poet.

Nomi Stone, "Drones: An Exercise in Awe-Terror" from *Tahoma Literary Review*. Reprinted by permission of the poet.

Adrienne Su, "Peaches" from The Academy of American Poets' Poem-a-Day feature. Reprinted by permission of the poet.

James Tate, "Dome of the Hidden Temple" from *Dome of the Hidden Pavilion*. Reprinted by permission of Ecco/HarperCollins. Also appeared in *jubilat*.

Lee Upton, "The Apology" from *The New Yorker*. Reprinted by permission of the poet.

C. K. Williams, "Hog" from *Selected Later Poems*. Reprinted by permission of Farrar, Straus and Giroux. Also appeared in *The New Yorker*.

Eleanor Wilner, "To Think of How Cold" from *New Ohio Review*. Reprinted by permission of the poet.

Al Young, "The Drummer Omar: Poet of Percussion" from *Brilliant Corners*. Reprinted by permission of the poet.